Southern Lady

GRACIOUS TABLES

Southern Lady
GRACIOUS TABLES
{ THE PERFECT SETTING FOR ANY OCCASION }

PHYLLIS HOFFMAN

Collins

An Imprint of HarperCollinsPublishers

Author: Phyllis Hoffman
Editor: Barbara Cockerham
Associate Editor: Stacey Norwood
Staff Writer: Amanda Manning
Test Kitchen Director: Rebecca Treadwell Touliatos
Food Editors: Aimee Bishop, Loren Wood
Copy Editor: Lucas Whittington
Creative Director: Mac Jamieson
Style Director: Yukie McLean
Photographers: Marcy Black, Kimberly Finkel Davis, Arden Ward
Photo Stylist: Lindsay Keith Kessler
Art Director: Karissa Brown
Illustrators: Marie Barber, Zen Chuang
Color Technicians: Delisa McDaniel, Chris Waits
Production Director: Greg Baugh

HarperCollins books may be purchased for educational, business, or sales
promotional use. For information please write: Special Markets Department,
HarperCollins Publishers Inc., 10 East 53rd Street, New York, NY 10022.

FIRST EDITION

Library of Congress Cataloging-in-Publication Data has been applied for.
ISBN 10: 0-06-134667-5
ISBN: 978-0-06-134667-5

07 08 09 10 9 8 7 6 5 4 3 2 1

{ DEDICATION }

This book is dedicated to the women in my life who inspire me daily.

To my mother, Inez Norton, who has been my role model my entire life. Your creativity is amazing and your way of making simple things elegant with your touch continually inspires me. God selected you just for me.

To my sister, Janice Ritter, who always has a theme for every holiday and makes birthdays last for weeks. Hospitality is your gift and you share it with everyone around you. God selected you just for me.

To my dear friend Barbara Cockerham, who makes each day beautiful with perfectly chosen words of encouragement and love. You are a gifted writer and you continually amaze me with your insight into life. God selected you just for me.

To Lorna Reeves, whom I love like a daughter. Watching you grow into a very accomplished young woman, wife and mother has been delightful. You always find the good in everyone and love unconditionally. God selected you just for me.

To Katie Miller Hoffman, my first daughter-in-law. From the day I met you, I knew that you would be the perfect mate for my son. I adore you more than you will ever know and look forward to our new life together. God selected you for me.

To Yukie McLean, the most creative person I know. Your friendship is a treasure, your talents astonishing and your sweet heart is always refreshing. God selected you for me.

To each of you, I love you so much. God selected each one of you for a specific place in my life and in my heart. *GRACIOUS TABLES* is about beautiful settings that make a backdrop for the people we love. You are the women who make my life beautiful.

{ CONTENTS }

INTRODUCTION

{ THE SOUTHERN LADY AT HOME }
Gracious Tables, Past and Present

Set a gracious table. What do these words mean to you? To me, that sentence is ripe with context, cherished memories, and simple joy. Why? Because so many of the most important moments of my life have taken place around a kitchen or dining room table—little heartbeats of time that, ultimately, have led me along some extraordinary paths, both personally and professionally.

It was around a table that my career in publishing was born. When I entered my friend Barbara Cockerham's house in Cullman, Alabama, for the first time, I was immediately enamored of the colorful cross stitch pieces I saw hanging on her walls. I asked her to teach me this art form, one that combined my love of textiles, artistry, and precision needlework; she readily agreed.

As Barbara tutored me in cross stitching around her kitchen table, our friendship grew, and with it a mutual desire to seek out magazine resources for our hobby. To our surprise, there were none. With a background in business, I knew a niche when I saw one, and with her expertise in journalism, Barbara knew how to make our wish for a needlework magazine a reality. *Just CrossStitch* was the first magazine ever published by Hoffman Media, but not the last. *Southern Lady, Cooking With Paula Deen, TeaTime,*

*A peek into my cupboard
is a peek into my life.
It tells of the wonderful
gifts I have received from
loved ones, of pieces I
have inherited, and of the
beautiful things that have
spoken to me over the years.*

—PHYLLIS HOFFMAN

Taste of the South, and several others were to come, all thanks to the therapy of stitching and laughter enjoyed with my best friend at her table so many years ago.

Of course, my own dining table has always been a source of personal beauty and comfort to me. As a Southern lady by birth and by nature, my love of entertaining is almost inborn. My mother was my greatest mentor in appreciating and creating great tablescapes for all occasions, great and small. A painter and artist herself, my mom, through her own talents and skills, taught me the importance of color, composition, and texture—these are the building blocks of creating a breathtaking table.

Using the skills she taught me, combined with an infinite love of beautiful things—especially fine china—I have prepared many a table for many an occasion. When guests come to my home for a dinner party, luncheon, afternoon tea, or other event, one of the questions that is inevitably asked of me is "Just how many sets of china do you have?" I always look at them very coyly and ask, "Why? Do you have one I need?"

I love collecting, but more than that, I love making use of my collections. My philosophy is, if it breaks, it's broken. But if you miss an occasion, you've missed an opportunity. I also believe that creating a beautiful environment for yourself, your family, and your guests is one of the most important tasks of a woman and hostess. And, of course, setting a gracious table is not just about the china. It's also about creating a comforting environment, one that inspires your guests to feel at ease and be themselves, to relax and enter into a conversation that is meaningful for all.

To that end, I invite you to visit with me in my own home, as well as the homes of a few friends as, together, we explore the timeless art of setting a gracious table, and all that those words imply.

OPPOSITE: The first set of china I ever purchased was blue and white, and I love it still. My collection today includes such pieces as reproduction spice jars and decorative canisters—even a punch bowl. The sharply contrasting but simple color scheme makes mixing and matching numerous combinations of patterns in blue and white an easy task.

Tip: Canadian bacon glazed with a little barbecue sauce is the perfect marriage of flavor and convenience. It's cooked and ready for the table or a chafing dish in less than 10 minutes. If you like, spiral or even thickly sliced honey ham may be substituted. Just don't use Virginia or country ham; both are too salty for the barbecue sauce.

FRUIT SALAD WITH LIME-MINT DRESSING
Yield: 8 servings

1	cup mint jelly
2	tablespoons honey
1	tablespoon lime zest
3	tablespoons lime juice
2	apples, cut into bite-size pieces
1/2	fresh pineapple, cut into bite-size pieces
1	cup red seedless grapes
1	cup green seedless grapes
1/2	cantaloupe, cut into bite-size pieces
1/2	honeydew, cut into bite-size pieces

1. In a microwave-safe bowl, microwave jelly on High for approximately one minute. Whisk in honey, lime zest and juice until well blended.
2. In a large bowl, combine apples, pineapple, grapes, cantaloupe, and honeydew. Pour the lime-mint dressing over the mixed fruit. Chill before serving.

CANADIAN BACON ROUNDS
Yield: 6 servings

1/4	cup butter, melted
12	slices Canadian bacon
1/4	cup barbecue sauce

1. In a medium sauté pan over medium heat, melt butter. Cook Canadian bacon slices, stirring constantly for 2 to 3 minutes, or until lightly browned.
2. Pour barbecue sauce over Canadian bacon and cook until heated through.

• • • • •

If mint isn't to your taste, use orange marmalade in place of the mint jelly for the fruit salad. Apricot or peach would also work well.

Tip: To save time, prepare cheese grits the night before—leaving off the extra sprinkle of cheese and bits of bacon until ready to pop in the oven.

BACON AND CHEESE GRITS
Yield: 8 to 12 servings

1½ cups grits, uncooked
3   cups grated Cheddar cheese
3   eggs, beaten
⅓   cup milk
¼   teaspoon ground red pepper, or to taste
5   slices bacon, cooked and crumbled, divided

1. Preheat oven to 375°.
2. Cook grits on stovetop according to package directions. Remove from heat.
3. Add 2 cups cheese, eggs, milk, ground red pepper, and 3 slices crumbled bacon; stir well.
4. Pour into a buttered 3-quart baking dish. Top with remaining cheese and crumbled bacon. Bake for 20 minutes.

BLUEBERRY-PIE FRENCH TOAST
Yield: 6 servings

4   ounces cream cheese, softened
½   cup blueberry pie filling
12   slices Texas toast bread
8   eggs
1   cup milk

1. In a small bowl, combine cream cheese and pie filling. Spread 1 side of six bread slices evenly with cream-cheese mixture. Top with remaining bread slices, cream-cheese sides together, to create six sandwiches.
2. Fit sandwiches into a separate baking dish in a single layer.
3. In a small bowl, whisk together eggs and milk. Pour over sandwiches. Cover and chill for at least 30 minutes, turning sandwiches once.
4. Preheat oven to 400°. Lightly grease a 13x9x2-inch baking dish.
5. Place sandwiches in a single layer in prepared baking dish, discarding any excess egg mixture.
6. Bake for 20 to 25 minutes, or until lightly browned. Serve with strawberry or other desired syrup.

MEMORABLE MOMENTS

CREATING AN UNFORGETTABLE OCCASION FOR THE SPECIAL PEOPLE IN YOUR LIFE BEGINS WITH CATERING TO THEIR TASTES.

As a mother of twin sons, I realize I am doubly blessed. I love my children fiercely, and there is little I wouldn't do for my boys, but birthdays have always been a bit of a challenge. Not just because Eric and Brian are twins—meaning there are two cakes, two of every present, and two sets of candles for birthday wishes—but also, more simply, because they're boys.

Girls? Easy, easy. Girls love frilly and fun, and even those who don't tend to respond in some innately feminine way to a beautifully set table with pretty china and fresh flowers. But boys? Now that's a horse of a different color entirely. For birthdays and homecomings, you must create a table that is pretty without being…"pretty." Easier said than done.

Perhaps it is my love of textiles, but I've never been able to bring myself to throw out or give away a silk tie after my boys outgrew it. And I finally found a use for them—I used the ties as the basis for a tablescape for a get-together for my sons and their friends. Arrayed around the circumference of the table and anchored by the centerpiece—made of live goldfish no less—the ties added color, texture, and verve. A menu of my boys' favorite dishes, including Mom's baked spaghetti, worked with the dressed-up but still casual look and tone of the evening.

Tip: If you don't have enough ties to finish the table, visit a thrift store or jumble sale. You should find an ample supply. Just be sure to have them dry-cleaned before using.

BAKED SPAGHETTI
Yield: 8 servings

1   pound ground chuck
1   pound ground Italian sausage
2   cloves garlic, minced
1   green bell pepper, chopped
1   yellow onion, chopped
1   (28-ounce) can crushed tomatoes
1   (8-ounce) can tomato sauce
1   (6-ounce) can tomato paste
1   teaspoon dried oregano
1   teaspoon dried basil leaves
1   teaspoon sugar
8   ounces uncooked linguine pasta
1   (16-ounce) container sour cream
1   (8-ounce) package cream cheese, softened
½   cup chopped green onion
2   cups shredded Colby-Jack cheese blend

1. In a Dutch oven, brown ground chuck, sausage, garlic, bell pepper, and onion over medium-high heat, until meat crumbles and vegetables are tender; drain.
2. Stir in crushed tomatoes, tomato sauce, tomato paste, oregano, basil and sugar. Reduce heat and simmer, 30 minutes.
3. Cook pasta according to package directions, draining well.
4. Preheat oven to 350°.
5. Place pasta in individual baking dishes or a 13x9x2-inch baking dish.
6. In a small bowl, combine sour cream, cream cheese, and green onion. Spread evenly over hot pasta. Top with meat sauce.
7. Bake 20 to 25 minutes, or until heated. Sprinkle with cheese, and bake an additional 5 minutes, or until cheese is melted.

• • • • •

Baked spaghetti is a meal in itself, needing little in the way of sides. Garlic or cheese breadsticks plus an easy-does-it tossed green salad are plenty.

S'MORES BROWNIES A LA MODE
Yield: 2 dozen

1   family-size brownie mix (yields a 9x13-inch pan of brownies)
10 whole graham cracker squares, broken into pieces
2   cups miniature marshmallows
1   cup milk chocolate chips
Vanilla ice cream
Caramel ice cream topping

1. Preheat oven to 350°. Lightly grease a 13x9x2-inch baking pan.
2. Prepare brownie mix according to package directions. Pour into prepared pan. Bake 18 minutes.
3. Remove from oven. Sprinkle with graham cracker pieces, pressing down lightly. Sprinkle evenly with marshmallows and chocolate chips. Return to oven, and continue baking 12 minutes. Cool, and cut into 24 squares.
4. To serve, place brownie square on serving plate, cover with scoop of vanilla ice cream and drizzle with caramel sauce.

• • • • •

S'Mores Brownies are delicious by themselves, but just plain heavenly when paired with ice cream and a generous drizzle of buttery caramel sauce. If you prefer, or even just to save time, crumble or break the brownies into pieces and place in parfait or sundae glasses. Top with scoops of ice cream along with caramel or chocolate sauce for a sweet finish.

FORMAL AFFAIR

A FORMAL FAMILY MEAL OR DINNER PARTY WITH FRIENDS CALLS FOR A MENU THAT WILL SATISFY EVEN THE MOST FINICKY PALATE.

I spent years searching for a formal dining room table, and I wouldn't trade it for any other. It is round, seats 10 easily and 12 with effort, and is a glorious 88-inches in diameter. Everyone who sits at my table feels special, because no one seat upstages the other. No one is ever left out of a conversation, and there is ample room to create a beautiful tablescape.

When my table is set with fine china for a fancy to-do or ta-da—and mind you, it might just be a plate of a different pattern at every seat—I am happiest. I love taking the time and trouble to entertain, to make others feel welcome and special, then send them home with their appetites for good food, good company, and great conversation thoroughly satiated. For your own sit-down occasions, try one of my favorite can't-fail dinner menus. It's easier to prepare than it looks, and for dessert? A quintessential Southern sweet—red velvet cake.

OPPOSITE: Lovely embroidered linens add an elegant touch to an already stunning formal table.

PARMESAN AND HERB-STUFFED MUSHROOMS
Yield: 4 dozen

48 mushrooms
1/4 cup butter, melted
3/4 cup grated Parmesan cheese
1 (8-ounce) package cream cheese, softened
1/4 cup sour cream
2 cloves garlic, minced
1 tablespoon minced fresh parsley
2 tablespoons minced fresh thyme
3 tablespoons fresh lemon juice

1. Preheat oven to 350°.
2. Remove stems from mushrooms. Wipe caps clean with a damp paper towel.
3. Brush mushrooms with melted butter and place in a 13x9x2-inch baking dish.
4. Combine remaining ingredients until well blended. Pipe evenly into mushroom caps. Bake for 20 to 25 minutes, or until lightly golden.

BACON-WRAPPED FIGS
Yield: 2 dozen

24 dried figs, stems removed
8 slices bacon, cut into thirds
1/2 cup soy sauce
2 tablespoons dark brown sugar
2 tablespoons fresh lemon juice

1. Preheat oven to 350°. Line baking sheet with aluminum foil.
2. Wrap each fig with one-third slice bacon and secure with a toothpick.
3. In a small bowl, mix together soy sauce, brown sugar, and lemon juice. Dip each bacon-wrapped fig into sauce, coating well.
4. Place on prepared sheet pan and bake for 20 minutes, or until bacon is crispy. Serve warm.

Tip: With any cream sauce, you run the risk of curdling if not careful. As soon as the sauce begins to thicken, remove from heat.

GRILLED BEEF TENDERLOIN
Yield: 12 servings

1   (6-pound) beef tenderloin, trimmed
3   tablespoons coarse-ground black pepper
1   (10-ounce) bottle white-wine Worcestershire sauce
1   recipe Brandied Mushroom Sauce (recipe follows)

1. Preheat grill to medium-high heat (350° to 400°).
2. Rub tenderloin with pepper. Place tenderloin in a shallow dish or heavy-duty zip-top plastic bag; add Worcestershire sauce. Cover or seal, and chill for at least 3 hours.
3. Remove tenderloin, discarding marinade.
4. Grill tenderloin, covered with lid, over direct heat for 10 minutes, turning once. Reduce heat to medium-low (250° to 300°), and grill, covered with lid, for 40 minutes, or until desired doneness, turning every 10 minutes. Remove from grill.
5. Cover loosely with aluminum foil, and let stand for 15 minutes before slicing.
6. Serve with Brandied Mushroom Sauce.

BRANDIED MUSHROOM SAUCE
Yield: 2½ cups

1   (8-ounce) package whole mushrooms, quartered
2   cloves garlic, minced
4   green onions, thinly sliced
4   tablespoons butter
¼   cup brandy
1   tablespoon all-purpose flour
¼   teaspoon salt
¼   teaspoon ground black pepper
⅔   cup heavy cream

1. In a medium saucepan, cook mushrooms, garlic, and onion in butter, stirring constantly for 3 minutes over medium-high heat on stovetop. Add brandy; cook for 3 minutes.
2. Stir in flour, salt, and pepper; cook for 1 minute.
3. Stir in cream; cook for approximately 3 minutes until thickened.

Tip: I love to dress up vegetables with ingredients that enhance both the flavor and the presentation. Pecans and a little sweet teriyaki sauce make green beans sing!

SAUTÉED GREEN BEANS WITH PECANS
Yield: 8-10 servings

¼ cup olive oil
1 (2-pound) bag frozen cut green beans, thawed
2 teaspoons sugar
1 teaspoon salt
½ teaspoon black pepper
⅓ cup Teriyaki sauce
3 tablespoons butter
1 cup chopped pecans

1. Warm sauté pan on high heat. Add olive oil. Add beans to hot oil and cook, stirring constantly until beans begin to lightly brown.
2. Add sugar, salt, pepper, and Teriyaki sauce and continue to cook for 2 to 3 minutes.
3. Add butter to pan. When butter is melted, stir in pecans. Cook, stirring constantly for 2 to 3 minutes.

SWISS TARRAGON POTATOES
Yield: 10-12 servings

1 (5-pound) bag Yukon Gold potatoes
½ cup heavy cream
2 teaspoons salt
¾ teaspoon pepper
¼ cup chopped fresh tarragon
1½ cups grated Swiss cheese

1. Preheat oven to 400°. Butter a 13x9x2-inch baking dish.
2. Peel potatoes and slice thinly. Toss potatoes in a bowl with heavy cream, salt, and pepper.
3. Layer potatoes, tarragon, and cheese in prepared baking dish. Repeat layers twice, ending with cheese.
4. Bake for 45 to 50 minutes, or until potatoes are tender.

RED VELVET CAKE
Yield: 1 (8-inch) cake

3¾ cups all-purpose flour
2¼ cups sugar
⅓ cup plus 2 tablespoons cocoa powder
1½ teaspoons baking soda
1½ teaspoon salt
3 large eggs, lightly beaten
2¼ cups vegetable oil
1½ cups buttermilk
1½ teaspoons distilled white vinegar
1½ teaspoons vanilla extract
1 (1-ounce) bottle red food coloring
1 recipe Cream-Cheese Icing (recipe follows)

1. Preheat oven to 350°. Lightly grease and flour 3 (8-inch) cake pans.
2. In a mixing bowl, sift together flour, sugar, cocoa powder, baking soda, and salt.
3. Add eggs, oil, buttermilk, vinegar, vanilla extract, and red food coloring; beat at medium speed with electric mixer until combined.
4. Divide batter evenly among prepared cake pans.
5. Bake 35 minutes, or until a tester inserted near center comes out clean.
6. Let cool in pan 10 minutes. Remove cakes from pan, and cool completely on wire racks.
7. Spread Cream Cheese Icing between the layers and on sides and top of cake. Garnish with any additional crumb, if desired.

CREAM-CHEESE ICING
Yield: 5 cups

1 cup butter, softened
1 (8-ounce) package cream cheese, softened
2 teaspoons vanilla extract
1 (2-pound) package confectioners' sugar

In a large bowl, beat butter and cream cheese together with an electric mixer until creamy. Beat in vanilla extract. Gradually beat in confectioners' sugar, until desired consistency is reached.

{ PREPARING THE TABLE }

The Elements of Graciousness

Sweet courtesy has done its most if you have made each guest forget that he himself is not the host.

—THOMAS BAILEY ALDRICH

What defines graciousness? According to the dictionary, the word implies courtesy and kind consideration. It can also be described as "characterized by charm, good taste, generosity, and the tasteful leisure of good breeding." All of those things are true, but in the South, at least, graciousness is more than a mere word—it is a way of living, aimed at bringing about elevation of body, mind, and spirit. This translates to our tables through the time and care we take not only in arranging pretty place settings, but also in creating memorable celebrations with our families, our friends, our neighbors, and yes, sometimes just for ourselves. I believe there is inspiration to be found in every occasion, making the serving of a simple bowl of soup as worthy of my time and effort as a formal dinner party for twelve, or a Christmas dinner with all the relatives in tow. When my guests and loved ones sit at my table, I want them to feel a sense of interlude, a pleasant lull that stills the spirit, relaxes the body, and refreshes the mind. I do so not only by paying attention to the china, the silver, and the crystal, but also to the deeper meaning of the moment. By doing the same, you can fashion not only a gracious table, but a gracious life.

34

"MAGNOLIA AND BIRD" WATERCOLOR, BY ZEN CHUANG

{ SOUTHERN HOSPITALITY }

Some words I have always taken to heart are, "Be not forgetful to entertain strangers, for thereby some have entertained angels unawares." This, to me, is the very essence of Southern hospitality—a cordial combination that requires a sense of poise and unimpeachable courtesy. Whenever I entertain, I want everyone to feel a sense of welcome and warmth in my home, and I take pride in leaving no detail unattended. Blessings flow from many fountains, and those that are shared with others are pure joy.

36

SPRING CELEBRATION

USE THE QUIET SPLENDOR OF SPRING AS YOUR SOURCE OF INSPIRATION
WHEN PULLING TOGETHER AN AL FRESCO LUNCHEON FOR FRIENDS.

In the South, we are not only creatures of habit and tradition, but we are bound by season as well. From the starkness of winter to the abundance of summer, we celebrate every nuance of each passing month, taking dearly to heart the words "to every thing there is a season, a time to every purpose under heaven."

One of my favorite seasons has always been spring, and I often entertain on the spur of the moment, calling friends over for an impromptu springtime luncheon on the patio.

With little prep time to spare, I look to the landscape to shape my table design. An intimate table for four is perfect for the patio and promotes a sisterly sense of occasion while prompting ease of conversational flow. Since the food will be light (and last-minute), I like to dress up the occasion with crisp linens, delicate floral china, and aged heirloom silver.

The innocence of the color scheme mirrors the gentle charm of a lovely spring afternoon, while soft accents—such as lacy antique doilies used in lieu of underplates for soup bowls—add a genteel note of innovation. An unfussy bouquet adds a hint of color and bathes the scene in softness.

THE HOSPITALITY TRAY

WOW GUESTS WHO STAY IN YOUR HOME BY PREPARING A GRACIOUS "HOSPITALITY TRAY."

What lies at the heart of the rightfully famed Southern hospitality is genuine care for the comfort of others. This is never more necessary than when out-of-town or overnight guests stay in your home.

If you want to make a lasting impression when company drops in, set a hospitality tray for bedside service as guests arrive. A pot of coffee, a sweet or savory treat, and fresh flowers offer visitors a sense of welcome, while affording them a bit of much-needed privacy as they settle in.

Just remember, a hospitality tray is a sort of "mini table" and the same sense of aesthetics applies. Balance is key—a stately silver coffee pot takes center stage on the tray seen here. Delicate china cups sit atop dessert-sized plates that are perfect for enjoying a light muffin or scone. Linens are a must, of course, and monogrammed napkins add a note of sophistication to match the fine silver. A monogrammed napkin is always folded to showcase the monogram, and for this reason, napkin rings are neither used nor necessary.

A simple spray of red roses cut from the garden provides the perfect finishing touch, and more subtly, is in tonal harmony with the color scheme of the bedroom.

I collect beautifully monogrammed linens regardless of the initialing. Monograms originated in the Middle Ages, and were used as a means of identifying personal linens. Embroidered monograms were soon adopted by the aristocracy as a means of displaying personal pride in the family name.

Here is another tray that blends nicely with the color and decorative scheme of the guest room to which it is delivered. The ivory china and coffee pot echo the pristine bed linens, while the gently worn wicker serving tray is in keeping with the cozy cottage appeal of the room's furnishings. A simple lacy place mat is used to line the tray, which is set with the charming china, simple greenery, and an etched crystal vase. These almost imperceptible details make the gesture seem even more gracious.

RIGHT: The primary purpose of the hospitality tray is to make your guests feel cared for. Make sure you ask beforehand their preference of beverage—some may choose hot tea over coffee, or juice—as well as food likes and dislikes. It's also a nice touch to tuck in little extras, like a newspaper or even stationery and a fountain pen.

SOUTHERN STYLE

A GARDENSIDE TABLE HITS THE SPOT WHEN A SERVING OF FRESH TOMATOES IS ON THE MENU.

Is there anything more luscious, more delicious, more scandalously succulent than a juicy ripe tomato plucked fresh from the vine? In the South, we will take our tomatoes anywhere and any way we can get them, whether they're salted and sandwiched between two slices of white bread slathered in mayo, or quartered and tossed with garden fresh greens. In my family, my father's tomato garden has always been his pride and joy. As a child, I would prowl about the vines in search of just the right tomato, pluck it, and eat it like an apple. Today, as an adult, I still love to sneak tomatoes from Daddy's garden— green ones. If you haven't tried our famous fried green tomatoes, now is the time. Your summer dinner table isn't complete without them!

OPPOSITE: As with gardening, creating a summery, sunny tablescape requires the proper tools. Colorful crockery sets the tone, while potted flowers—rather than a bouquet—are in keeping with the spirit of the season. A basket filled with fresh fruit adds another layer of color and shape to the overall design.

There's nothing more beautiful than morning mist.
It's almost magical…

—PHYLLIS HOFFMAN

Tip: As any old hand in the kitchen can tell you, one of the challenges of preparing fried green tomatoes is frying them without losing the precious cornmeal batter that gives the dish its signature salty crunch. Try frying the battered tomatoes in a shallow pan of oil and cook only a few at a time.

48

FRIED GREEN TOMATOES
Yield: 4 servings

1½ cups all-purpose flour, divided
3/4 cup yellow cornmeal
1   teaspoon salt, divided
1   teaspoon ground black pepper, divided
3   large eggs
3/4 cup buttermilk
1½ cups canola oil
4   green tomatoes, sliced into 12 (½-inch-thick) slices
Crab and Green Chile Cream Sauce (recipe follows)
Garnish: crumbled bacon, grape tomatoes, sliced green onion

1. Spoon 3/4 cup flour into a shallow dish and set aside. Combine remaining flour, cornmeal, ½ teaspoon salt, and ½ teaspoon pepper in a separate shallow dish. Whisk eggs with buttermilk and pour into a separate shallow dish. In a 10-inch nonstick skillet, heat canola oil over medium-high heat.
2. Evenly sprinkle each tomato slice with ½ teaspoon salt and ½ teaspoon pepper. Dust tomato slices in flour, dip in buttermilk mixture, and dredge in flour and cornmeal mixture. Fry tomato slices, one at a time, for 3 to 4 minutes on each side, or until lightly browned and tomato is tender.
3. To assemble, stack three tomatoes and top with Crab and Green Chile Cream Sauce. Garnish with crumbled bacon, grape tomatoes, and sliced green onions, if desired.

• • • • •

Another tip for perfectly fried green tomatoes: make sure the cooking oil is heated on medium-high. This ensures that tomatoes will cook evenly. Also, cooking time can vary slightly with different tomatoes— some simply cook quicker than others, so test each slice with a fork for tenderness. Naturally firm when uncooked, fried green tomatoes should feel as tender as ripe tomatoes when pierced with a fork.

Tip. Vine-ripened tomatoes are perfect for fresh garden salsa. Just mix together chopped tomatoes, fresh cilantro and red onion to taste, and one or two seeded, diced jalapenos. For extra flavor, add black beans or drained canned corn. Delicious!

CRAB AND GREEN CHILE CREAM SAUCE
Yield: about 3 cups

2	tablespoons butter
1/4	cup chopped yellow onion
1/4	cup chopped green bell pepper
1	tablespoon garlic
1	(4.5-ounce) can chopped green chiles-drained
1	cup chicken stock
1/2	teaspoon salt
1/4	teaspoon cayenne pepper
1/4	teaspoon Cajun seasoning
2	cups heavy cream
1	(8-ounce) can white crabmeat

1. In a saucepan, melt butter over medium-high heat. Add onion, bell pepper, and garlic; cover and cook for 3 minutes or until tender.
2. Stir in green chiles, chicken stock, salt, cayenne pepper, and Cajun seasoning; cook for 5 minutes.
3. Stir in cream and crabmeat; cook for approximately 8 to 10 minutes, or until thickened.

• • • • •

Fried Green Tomatoes with Crab and Green Chile Sauce is a variation on another Southern classic developed at the renowned Upperline Restaurant in New Orleans. After seeing the famous movie of the same name, the restaurant's owner, JoAnne Clevenger was inspired to add fried green tomatoes to the menu at Upperline. She later paired the Southern delicacy with a Creole classic—shrimp rémoulade. The tartness of the tomatoes is a perfect counterpart for the tangy rémoulade sauce.

SOCIAL GRACES

IN THE SOUTH, MANNERS MATTER. HOSTING A LUNCHEON IS AN EXCELLENT OPPORTUNITY TO PRACTICE ETIQUETTE, AND THE PERFECT EXCUSE TO SET A PRETTY TABLE.

A true Southern lady is always in possession of three things: her sense of humor, at least one piece of her mother's jewelry, and her manners. In fact, as any Southern lady will surely tell you, even if the first two temporarily take their leave, the third will save you—in any number of situations.

Etiquette, like anything else, must be learned, and I have always believed that one of the best ways to teach is by example. A special luncheon or dinner is the best way I can think of to pass on and to practice the traditions and rules of etiquette to young men and women entering adulthood.

For such an occasion, the table should be intimate but beautiful, formal but not fussy. Precious china, embroidered linens, and fine crystal set the tone for the occasion, and details of the design scheme should be planned just as meticulously.

An uncluttered centerpiece of flowers lends a note of beauty without obstructing the view or flow of conversation, and the height of the bouquet balances the unique crystal glasses on the table. Pears perched in etched crystal sherbet dishes adorn an already gorgeous table with an unexpected bit of whimsy. And as a lovely grace note, sugary Jordan almonds nestled in silver wire-weave nut baskets make wonderful take-home keepsakes of such a special occasion.

{ MIND YOUR MANNERS }

Remember these basic rules of etiquette when passing along or brushing up on your own table manners.

- Cell phones should be turned off before seating begins. Answering telephone calls or sending text messages while dining with others is unspeakably rude.

- Know when to stand and when to sit. When chatting before dinner, gentlemen should stand when a lady enters the room and should not sit at the table before their female counterparts have done so. Once seated at the table, gentlemen are also expected to rise if a latecomer who is female enters the room. Both men and women should remain standing until the host or hostess is seated.

- Know your napkin etiquette. Wait until the hostess has placed her napkin in her lap before following suit, and if grace is to be said before the meal, leave your napkin in place until after the prayer is concluded. If you must leave the table during the meal, place your napkin in the seat of your chair. Also, use your napkin to blot—don't wipe. This is doubly true for women wearing lipstick. When the meal has ended, and after the hostess has done the same, place your napkin to the left of the plate.

- Learn the order of use. If you stumble across unfamiliar silverware pieces at your place setting—don't falter. The most basic rule is to start eating with those utensils on the outside and work your way in with each course. If you are still confused, quietly take note of when your hostess uses a particular utensil—and how.

- When passing food, salt and pepper, or other requested items to fellow diners, always pass to the right.

- Don't forget to compliment the hostess on her beautiful table, the delicious entree, or the divine dessert! Be sincere—don't claim to love a menu item you barely tasted—but find at least one positive aspect of the occasion, the company, or the meal to comment on before leaving.

- After the meal is over, don't rush out, but don't linger too long either. Most dinner or luncheon guests are expected to stay about an hour after the conclusion of the meal.

Manners are a sensitive awareness of the feelings of others. If you have that awareness, you have good manners, no matter which fork you use.

—EMILY POST

54

TEA TIME TRADITIONS

Though it has recently experienced a resurgence in popularity elsewhere in the United States, the old-fashioned tea party has never gone out of style in the South. I would hazard a guess that most young ladies here have hosted or attended a tea party at least once in their lifetime.

The occasions are many—a bridal tea, a baby shower, a birthday—but the simple celebration of afternoon tea is one of sheer graciousness, and with good reason. Tea forces us to slow down, both in the preparation and enjoyment of the beverage itself, and in the accoutrements and asides that accompany it. A tea sandwich made of crustless butter-glossed bread and paper-thin slices of cucumber is not meant to be consumed without thought; it is intended to be savored. Likewise, tea that is served in delicate bone china pots and cups should be sipped, slowly and with all the care such fine teawares demand.

OPPOSITE: A wooden arbor of roses provides a natural frame for the first view of your tea party setting. Rose petals strewn along the garden path add a refined touch, and guide guests to the table.

Strange how a teapot can represent at the same time the comforts of solitude and the pleasures of company.

—AUTHOR UNKNOWN

When hosting a tea party, it's fun to set a dazzling table. Weather permitting, a bountiful flower garden is a wonderful choice. Imagine your guests trodding along a brick-lined path, entering the garden gate, and spying a fully appointed table at path's end. What a sight!

Layered white linens will have the most visual impact, and are my favorite to collect. If you are starting your own collection, begin with damask table coverings that fit your table, then add linens for layering the look. For a tea party, try adorning each table in different sets and styles of linens. What fun!

Embellish your table with an array of teawares—sugar bowl, creamer, teapots, and more. Get creative—use a different tea set for every table and tie the tables together with a single, smashing centerpiece on each. In this case, a triple tier combination of orchids and roses with cascading wisps of greenery lends height, color, and balance to the table. Orchids are a particular favorite of mine; they are unforgettable flowers that bloom in a rainbow of colors—sometimes two or three shades in a single blossom—and are incredibly versatile to work with.

OPPOSITE: Orchids are tropical by nature; you can extend their vase life by misting daily with room-temperature water, and trimming stems at an angle every few days.

SOUTHERN SCRUMPTIOUS

SETTING THE SCENE FOR SUMMER IS A POINT OF PRIDE WITH SOUTHERN HOSTESSES. AND NO SUMMER TABLE WOULD BE COMPLETE WITHOUT A GLASS OF LEMONADE AND A PLATE OF BARBECUE.

It's hard to believe that the simple blend of lemons, water, and sugar can produce so remarkable a beverage, but if you've ever spent a summer in the South, you know just what I mean. Down here, it's not so much the sun's heat that will wilt you as the humidity.

On the other hand, a day spent indoors when the sun is shining its brightest is a day wasted, so we've learned to cope—with lots of lemonade. Of course, in the summertime—when as the great Gershwin put it, the "livin' is easy,"—we Southerners let our hair down a little. Entertaining moves from the formal dining room to the back yard, where we can relax and enjoy each other's company and the sunny scenery. That's not to say we don't like to set a sumptuous table, but the setting downshifts a bit to match the mood and surroundings.

Like every other Southern hostess I know, I invite friends and family over at least once each summer for a good, old-fashioned barbecue. Summertime in the South without barbecue is like Thanksgiving without a turkey—as we like to say, "it just ain't right." Smoky pulled pork dripping in tangy barbecue sauce makes the best sandwiches you can imagine, and of course, as with any barbecue, you can't skimp on the "sides." A cool slaw and chilled potato salad are perfect picks—washed down with glass after glass of lemonade, of course!

{ SUMMER BARBECUE }

White crockery on wicker chargers adds flair to the table, and can be accented by decorative wicker and glass accessories. Colorful cotton linens are in keeping with the casual theme and menu, and pop against the otherwise neutral tablescape.

NEW POTATO SALAD
Yield: 8 to 10 servings

1½ to 2 cups mayonnaise
1 cup sour cream
1 tablespoon prepared horseradish
2 tablespoons spicy mustard
1½ teaspoons celery seed
1 teaspoon salt
3 pounds boiled small, new potatoes, sliced ¼ inch thick
1 cup chopped fresh thyme, divided

1. In a small bowl, combine the mayonnaise, sour cream, horseradish, mustard, celery seed, and salt.
2. In a large bowl, combine potatoes and ½ cup thyme. Add mayonnaise mixture and combine until well blended.
3. Cover and chill 2 hours or overnight. Sprinkle with remaining ½ cup thyme prior to serving.

SOUTHERN HOSPITALITY SLAW
Yield: 8 servings

1 cup mayonnaise
¼ cup apple cider vinegar
¼ cup sugar
1 teaspoon salt
2 (16-ounce) packages tri-color cole slaw mix

1. In a medium bowl, combine mayonnaise, vinegar, sugar, and salt.
2. In a large bowl, combine mayonnaise mixture and slaw mix. Stir to combine. Cover and marinate 2 hours in refrigerator.

Tip: If you prefer to grill the pork for your sandwiches, butterfly the pork loin, then grill over medium hot coals for 20 to 25 minutes, or until a meat thermometer registers 160°. The pork will not shred, so slice thinly instead.

PULLED PORK BARBECUE SANDWICHES

Yield: 4-6 servings

1 (2-pound) boneless pork loin, trimmed
1/2 teaspoon salt
1/2 teaspoon ground black pepper
1/4 cup olive oil
3 cloves garlic
2 cups chicken broth
Bottled hickory smoked barbecue sauce
Dill pickle chips
4 to 6 hamburger buns

1. Cut pork loin in half length-wise; season with salt and pepper. In a Dutch oven, heat olive oil over medium-high heat. Add pork loin, browning all sides. Remove pork loin and in same pan, cook garlic for 1 to 2 minutes, stirring constantly. Return pork loin to pan; reduce heat to medium-low and add chicken broth. Cover and simmer for 1½ to 2 hours, until tender, turning meat every 30 minutes. Remove from heat and cool 10 minutes. With two forks, shred meat into bite size pieces.
2. To assemble sandwiches, layer pork, barbecue sauce, and pickles on buns, which can be steamed or buttered and toasted first, if desired.

• • • • •

Though barbecue sauce is used as a condiment on these sandwiches, it can also used to baste the meat if it is grilled. The version used here is thick and sweet, but homemade barbecue sauces vary in different parts of the South, from mustard-based to thin and more vinegary varieties.

LEMON-BLUEBERRY PARFAITS
Yield: 10 parfaits

2   cups sugar
1   cup butter
$^1/_2$ teaspoon fresh grated lemon zest
$^3/_4$ cup lemon juice
5   eggs, lightly beaten
1   small prepared angel-food cake
1   pint blueberries
1   (8-ounce) container frozen whipped topping, thawed
Garnish: additional blueberries and mint

1. Bring water to a boil in bottom-half of a 2-quart double boiler.
2. Combine sugar, butter, lemon zest, and lemon juice in top-half of double boiler. Reduce heat to low; cook until butter melts.
3. Gradually, stir about one-fourth of hot mixture into eggs to temper; add to remaining hot mixture, stirring constantly.
4. Cook, stirring constantly, for approximately 15 minutes, over simmering water until mixture thickens. Remove from heat; chill for 1 hour.
5. Cut or tear angel-food cake into 1-inch pieces. Divide one-third of the blueberries into 10 parfait glasses. Top with one-third of the cake pieces and one-third of the lemon curd. Repeat layers twice. Top each parfait with whipped topping. Garnish with additional blueberries and mint, if desired.

• • • • •

Lemon curd is the basis of these simple but heavenly trifle parfaits. Ever versatile, you can easily change the curd and fruit to suit your tastes. Try strawberries or raspberries instead of blueberries, and fresh orange or lime juice makes a sweet stand-in for the lemon.

{ HOME & HEARTH }

Gather 'round the table. We have a deep reverence for these words in the South, where such traditions as Sunday supper with the family are not only honored, but cherished. In my own life and in my own home, the family table is the table that matters most. Sometimes that is a cloth-covered picnic table with benches, and other times that means a breakfast counter set with fine china. No matter the location, wherever my family is, that's the family table.

DOWN HOME

A family picnic on the farm doesn't mean skimping on pretty details for the table. Rather, rise to the occasion with a design scheme that reflects the rural scenery and adds to the fun factor.

An oversized hand-pieced quilt has country charm to spare and provides a colorful canvas upon which to create your picnic tablescape. Sturdy square stoneware and ceramic

RIGHT: One of the benefits of using a hefty quilt as a table covering is that it will stay put even on the windiest afternoon.

dinnerware adorned with farm-friendly critters lend a playful element. Dishwasher-safe flatware and drinking glasses are just fine—this is not a table that begs for fine crystal—while plump pillows at each place setting invite family members to sit for a while.

Linens tied with lengths of raffia instead of napkin rings and a centerpiece that stretches nearly the length of the hand-hewn table are festive accents. Old tin lanterns from the barn balanced by bits of evergreen add height and woodsy fragrance, and are paired with vintage enamelware pitchers filled with leafy, berry-filled branches snipped in a jiffy from a nearby shrub.

RIGHT: If you don't have a quilt suitable in size or style for covering your picnic table, try using a bit of old-fashioned creativity instead. Overlap and layer printed tablecloths in vintage patterns; the cheerful and colorful prints from the 1950s are kitschy and cute—perfect for a picnic table. Enhance the effect by replacing napkins with dish towels from the same era.

RUSTIC CHARM

WITH A LITTLE IMAGINATION AND A KETTLE FILLED WITH HOT APPLE
CIDER, EVEN A WAGON SEAT CAN SERVE AS A FABULOUS TABLE FOR AN
AFTERNOON BEVERAGE BREAK.

I adore autumn. The range and intensity of the fall palette are pure inspiration—deep crimson and ochre, spicy shades of orange, earthy greens—all are brilliant and beautiful to me. Just the thought of those radiant hues makes me want to get outside to see them, preferably in the company of a loved one with a steaming cup of hot mulled cider to ward off the afternoon chill.

As with anything, of course, presentation is everything. A table, by definition, is any surface used for serving, so look around your yard and see what might work. In this case, the spring-raised seat of an old buckboard boasts not only irresistible charm, but just enough room for a wooden tray filled with a copper kettle for the hot beverage, earthenware mugs to hold the drink's heat, napkins, and even a few portly pumpkins for sheer effect.

ABOVE: Flea markets can yield any number of treasures, from antique copper kettles to lovely old wooden trays. Be prepared to arrive early and stay late—that's when you'll find the best bargains.

TIMELESS APPEAL

I have always held a deep affinity for history and personal heritage. Even my honeymoon was spent in Williamsburg, Virginia, where so many of our national traditions were born and so much of our American ancestry was shaped. I loved seeing that history in the cultural context that Williamsburg has so brilliantly crafted and preserved.

It seemed to me, and still does, that the gorgeous furniture, the amazingly creative needlework samplers, and of course, the home furnishings and tablewares of the Colonial age, were not only historically relevant, but also illustrate the very definition of artistry and fine craftsmanship.

Because of the annual seminars hosted by my needlework magazines, I still return to Williamsburg every fall following Thanksgiving, and each time I seem to discover some new exquisite thing to admire. Though my tastes have grown to include other styles over the years, I retain a deep fondness for early Americana. The evolution of the family dining table as we know it today in the United States started hundreds of years ago in the colonies, and amazingly, so little, and yet so much has changed in that time.

In the pre-Revolutionary period, tables weren't known as such, but rather boards—cupboards, groaning or hunt boards, table boards, etc. The main family meal, and the one presented with most flair and flourish, was dinner, typically served in early afternoon. As fortunes grew in the colonies, the dinner menus expanded.

Let not mercy and truth forsake thee. Bind them about thy neck.
Write them upon the tables of my heart.

—DESIER WILLIAMS
INSCRIPTION FROM NEEDLEWORK SAMPLER, 1756

Soups and "sallats," roasted meats, vegetables, relishes, sauces, bread, pies, and cakes—all required a means of serving and eating on the dining boards covered with linens that were likely spun, woven, and embroidered by the mothers and daughters of the house.

Platters, plates, bowls, tankards for drinking, and servingwares were most often made of sturdy pewter. These were both practical and decorative, as with porringers, handled shallow bowl-like dishes that came in an array of sizes, from two to nine inches in diameter. After the Revolution ended, and trade routes from the East opened up, porcelain and pottery soon replaced pewter in the collections of well-to-do wives.

Creamware, unadorned by color or motif, was perhaps the most popular, and remains a classic design style still emulated in today's china and pottery patterns. These enduring ivory and ecru pieces mix and match beautifully with many more modern styles. When beginning or adding to your own tableware collections, include these timeless styles, so that when the time comes, you can pass them on for new generations to enjoy.

MOTHER'S CHINA

I can still remember the first time I truly thought my mother was a glamorous Southern lady—when I saw our family's Franciscan *Ivy* china on "I Love Lucy." Imagine. My mother and Lucille Ball with the very same cups, saucers, and plates! Mom, in an act of generosity, gave me the set a few years ago because she knew I loved it. Today, when I pull those plates out of my own cupboard, I am reminded of happy times and wonderful family meals, such as my mother's heavenly "vegetable mix"—a crumbled layer of cornbread on the bottom, piled pyramid high with fresh corn, peas, fried okra, and chopped tomatoes on top. Though I don't pull out the set often, I do love to serve my own husband and children on those special plates. A table set with this popping pattern, updated by contemporary accents, such as jewel-toned glassware and modern beaded napkin rings, is one that positively glows.

KITCHEN COZY

REINVENT THE CONCEPT OF THE BREAKFAST BAR BY LOOKING AT THE UNUSUAL SPACE IN A DIFFERENT LIGHT.

How many of us have heard our mothers say breakfast is the most important meal of the day? Mother had a point. Not only is breakfast the fuel your body and mind need to greet the dawn of a new day, it's also an opportunity for families to spend some quality time together.

When my boys were young, I thought nothing of filling a hamper with my finest blue and white china on a whim, tucking in some muffins, juice, fruit, and other breakfast goodies, and heading for the park with my family for an impromptu picnic. The surroundings suited the casual tone the meal implied, but the china and juice goblets ratcheted up the elegance of the occasion. Those were memorable moments in my family's life, and times we will always remember together.

Now that my twins are older and living lives of their own, their visits are less frequent, and the time they do spend with Mom and Dad is precious. These days, I am more likely to prepare and serve breakfast at home, but I always try to convey the same mix of frivolity and care from those picnics of long ago at our current breakfast table—even if that table is not technically a table.

In today's kitchen styles, marble, granite, or wood-topped perimeter counters are more popular than ever, making for a

Life, within doors, has few pleasanter prospects than a neatly arranged and well-provisioned breakfast table.

—NATHANIEL HAWTHORNE

clever dual use of space. With stool seating, pretty china, flatware, linens, and a few other accents, the same marble countertop that serves as a workspace for preparing mouth-watering pastries can also double as a cozy breakfast nook.

The challenge of setting these "tables" is the narrow confines of the counter—there isn't the same depth a full table would allow for a cohesive design scheme. To overcome this, play to the length or width of the counter, dividing the visual line with unusal accent pieces at each place setting rather than a full-scale centerpiece. Pretty extras, like lidded glass canisters filled with fruit, potted plants or other greenery—anything that adds height to the linear look—make an impact without detracting from the close-quarters space.

84

RIGHT: Another secret to getting extra mileage out of a breakfast counter space—purchase and reserve one set of china just for this use, preferably something youthful and fun.

PROGRESSIVE SUPPER

Progressive suppers are always huge hits in the South—everyone starts with appetizers at one home and then they "progress" on to different homes for each subsequent course of the meal. It's not only a wonderful way to have a great time, but it's a fabulous excuse to show off our creativity and our unusual tablewares to each other. Why not try this with your family? Our menu of Southern comfort foods is to die for, starting with Southern Fried Egg Rolls and ending with a jazzed-up version of Praline Bread Pudding.

LEFT: The centerpiece of this Asian-inspired table is unique, yet so simple. Pretty bird figurines from a nearby shelf top a decorative wooden box, adding height and character. Flanked by flowers floating in a colorful vase, the centerpiece makes a powerful statement on the table.

{ STARTERS }

Southern Fried Egg Rolls are the perfect starter for a progressive supper. Inside the crispy shells are bits of bacon, pork tenderloin, and good old turnip greens. Of course, to keep the Southern flavor authentic, you have to kick them up a notch with a dash (or two, or three, or four) of hot sauce.

SOUTHERN FRIED EGG ROLLS
Yield: 15 servings

8	slices bacon
1/2	onion, finely chopped
1	clove garlic, minced
1	(1-pound) pork tenderloin, cut into 1-inch strips
1	(16-ounce) package frozen turnip greens, thawed and drained
1	(8-ounce) package cream cheese, softened
1/2	teaspoon hot sauce
1/4	teaspoon salt
1/4	teaspoon ground black pepper
1	(16-ounce) package egg roll wrappers

Vegetable oil for frying

1. In a large skillet, cook bacon over medium-high heat until crisp. Drain on paper towels, and crumble. Drain the skillet, reserving 2 tablespoons drippings in the pan. Add onion and garlic, and cook over medium-high heat 5 minutes, or until tender. Add pork, and cook 6 to 8 minutes or until done. Add turnip greens, and cook, stirring occasionally 5 minutes. Stir in cream cheese, hot sauce, salt, and pepper. Remove from heat, and let cool slightly.

2. Spoon 1/4 cup of the pork mixture on the bottom one-third of an egg roll wrapper. Fold the lower corner over filling, and roll it up, pausing to brush the left and right corners with water; fold corners toward center of filling. Brush top edge with water and roll up tightly. Repeat procedure for remaining filling and wrappers.

3. Fill a Dutch oven with 2 inches of oil; heat to 350°. Fry egg rolls in batches for 3 to 4 minutes, or until golden brown. Drain on paper towels.

Tip. The secret to perfect dumplings starts with the dough. Be sure not to over-knead or over-work the dough, else you'll end up with dumplings that are gummy and heavy, not light and fluffy.

{ SOUP COURSE }

At the second house on the tour of family homes, steaming bowls of chicken and dumpling soup is served. This stick-to-your ribs soup is a new take on a Southern favorite.

CHICKEN AND DUMPLINGS SOUP
Yield: 10 to 12 servings

2½ pounds split chicken breasts
10 black peppercorns
2   bay leaves
1   onion, sliced
1   rib celery, sliced
4   quarts water
1   (10.75-ounce) can cream of celery soup
1   (1-pound) package frozen mixed vegetables
2   teaspoons seasoned salt
¼   teaspoon salt
2   cups all-purpose flour
1   tablespoon baking powder
¾   teaspoon salt
1   cup milk
¼   cup butter

1. In a large Dutch oven, combine chicken, peppercorns, bay leaves, onion, celery, and water. Bring to a boil over medium-high heat; reduce heat, and simmer 45 minutes, or until chicken is tender. Remove chicken from broth; cool, remove skin and bones, and discard. Cut chicken into bite-sized pieces; set aside.

2. Strain broth, discarding solids. Return broth to Dutch oven. Stir in soup, vegetables, seasoned salt, and salt. Add chopped chicken. Bring to a boil over medium-high heat; reduce heat, and simmer 30 minutes.

3. In a small bowl, combine flour, baking powder, and salt. In a small micro-wave-safe bowl, combine milk and butter. Heat in microwave on HIGH in 30 second intervals, or until butter is melted. Stir warm milk mixture into flour mixture, mixing with a fork, just until combined. Drop dumplings by tablespoonfuls into simmering chicken broth mixture. Cover, and cook 15 to 20 minutes, or until dumplings are light and fluffy. Serve immediately.

Tip. Try serving these sweet potato biscuits with pepper jelly instead of orange honey butter. The red jelly is prettiest, and will give the biscuits and spiral sliced ham a sweet and spicy kick.

{ MAIN COURSE }

At the third house, heavier foods are served. Grits for supper? You bet—when it's fancied up in its Sunday best as a soufflé.

SWEET POTATO BISCUITS WITH HAM AND ORANGE HONEY BUTTER
Yield: about 1½ dozen

2½ cups all-purpose flour
¼   cup firmly packed brown sugar
1   tablespoon baking powder
½   teaspoon salt
¼   teaspoon ground cinnamon
½   cup butter, softened
1   cup mashed sweet potato
3½ tablespoons milk
Orange Honey Butter (recipe follows)
Spiral Sliced Honey Baked Ham

1. Preheat oven to 400°. Lightly grease baking sheet.
2. In a medium bowl, combine flour, brown sugar, baking powder, salt, and cinnamon. Cut in butter with a pastry blender until mixture is crumbly. Add sweet potato and milk, stirring with a fork until dry ingredients are moistened. Dough will be sticky.
3. Turn the dough onto a heavily floured surface, and knead lightly 4 or 5 times. Roll dough to ¾-inch thickness and cut biscuits with a 1¾-inch round cutter. Place on the prepared baking sheet. Bake 10 to 12 minutes, or until lightly browned. Serve with Orange Honey Butter and spiral sliced honey baked ham.

ORANGE HONEY BUTTER
Yield: about 1 cup

1   cup butter, softened
3   tablespoons orange marmalade
3   tablespoons honey

In a small bowl, beat butter with an electric mixer until fluffy. Beat in marmalade and honey. Serve at room temperature.

Tip: If you're not a huge fan of asparagus, try this substitute: use whole okra in its place. Prepare exactly the same as with the asparagus, except the cooking time, which should only differ by a minute or two.

FRIED ASPARAGUS WITH CREOLE MUSTARD SAUCE

Yield: 12 to 15 servings

1   pound fresh asparagus
1   cup all-purpose flour
1   cup whole buttermilk
1   large egg
1   tablespoon hot sauce
1½ cups self-rising cornmeal mix
2   tablespoons Cajun seasoning
Vegetable oil for frying
Creole Mustard Sauce (recipe follows)

1. Snap off the tough ends of the asparagus. Rinse asparagus with water, and leave damp. Place flour in a shallow dish, and dredge the damp asparagus in flour to coat.
2. In a shallow dish, whisk together buttermilk, egg, and hot sauce.
3. In another shallow dish, combine cornmeal mix and Cajun seasoning.
4. Dip asparagus in buttermilk mixture then dredge it in the cornmeal mixture.
5. Fill a Dutch oven with 2-inches of oil; heat to 365°. Fry asparagus, in batches, 4 to 5 minutes, or until golden brown. Drain on paper towels. Serve with Creole Mustard Sauce.

CREOLE MUSTARD SAUCE

Yield: about 1 cup

²/₃ cup sour cream
3   tablespoons Creole mustard
1½   teaspoons dry ranch dressing mix
1   teaspoon fresh lemon juice
¼   teaspoon Creole seasoning
¼   teaspoon onion powder
¼   teaspoon garlic powder

In a small bowl, combine all ingredients. Whisk until smooth. Cover and chill.

UPTOWN GRITS SOUFFLE
Yield: 6 to 8 servings

3½ cups water
½ teaspoon salt
¾ cup old-fashioned grits (not quick or instant)
2 cups grated fontina cheese
½ cup butter
1½ teaspoons minced garlic
½ teaspoon ground black pepper
2 large eggs
½ cup heavy cream

1. Preheat oven to 375°. Fill a 13x9x2-inch pan with 1 inch of hot water and place in oven. Grease an 8x8x2-inch baking dish; set aside.
2. In a large saucepan, bring water and salt to a boil over high heat. Stir in grits; reduce heat to low, cover and cook 20 minutes, stirring occasionally. Add cheese, butter, garlic, and pepper. Stir until butter and cheese are melted; remove from heat.
3. In a separate bowl, whisk together eggs and cream. Add egg mixture to grits mixture, mixing well. Spoon grits mixture into prepared pan. Cover with aluminum foil. Place in oven in center of 13x9x2-inch pan (water bath). Bake 15 minutes. Remove foil, and continue baking 20 minutes, or until set.

• • • • •

Another popular Southern dish made with grits, and one that is enduringly popular, is the combination of shrimp and grits. Usually served with creamy gravy, shrimp and grits is believed to have originated in South Carolina, where grits were adopted as the "official state food" in 1976. The state's official beverage? Sweet tea, of course.

Tip: When it comes to making bread pudding that will cut cleanly into individual portions, it's all about the bread. First, use day-old bread—it will soak up the custard without falling apart—and second, don't trim the crust from your bread, or you'll end up with a soggy mess.

{ FINALE }

The final stop in your Progressive Supper Party should include a little something for family members to take home—a remembrance of the occasion, wrapped in pretty boxes for each and every person who sits at the table. Of course, the real treat is the rich bread pudding, made with the flavors of one of our favorite confections in the South, pecan pralines.

PRALINE BREAD PUDDING WITH BOURBON SAUCE
Yield: 12 servings

2   (12-ounce) loaves French bread
1½ cups chopped pecans
½   cup butter, melted
1½ cups milk
1   cup heavy cream
¾   cup firmly packed dark brown sugar
½   cup sugar
½   cup caramel syrup
1   teaspoon vanilla extract
½   teaspoon rum extract
5   large eggs, lightly beaten
Bourbon Sauce (recipe follows)
Garnish: finely chopped pecans, confectioners' sugar

1. Preheat oven to 350°. Grease a 13x9x2-inch baking dish; set aside.
2. Cut bread into ½-inch cubes to measure 12 cups; place in a large mixing bowl. Reserve remaining bread for another use. Add pecans and butter to bread; toss gently. In a large saucepan, combine milk, cream, brown sugar, sugar, caramel syrup, and extracts. Bring to a simmer over medium heat, stirring frequently, until sugar dissolves.

{ RECIPE CONTINUES ON PAGE 100 }

3. Remove from heat. Whisking constantly, slowly add eggs to hot milk mixture until smooth. Pour custard mixture over bread mixture; let stand 10 minutes.

4. Pour bread mixture into prepared baking dish and place in another larger pan. Pour enough hot water into the larger pan to reach halfway up side of baking dish. Bake 45 minutes. Loosely cover with foil and bake 30 more minutes, or until custard is set and bread is golden brown. Remove from hot water bath. Let cool 30 minutes. Cut servings with a 2-inch round cutter. Serve warm with Bourbon Sauce. Garnish with chopped pecans and confectioners' sugar, if desired.

BOURBON SAUCE
Yield: 1½ cups

1   (14-ounce) can sweetened condensed milk
¼   cup bourbon
½   cup dark brown sugar
½   cup butter, cut into pieces
1   teaspoon vanilla extract

1. In a medium saucepan, combine condensed milk and bourbon. Bring to a simmer over medium heat, whisking constantly.

2. Add brown sugar and cook 1 to 2 minutes, whisking constantly, until mixture thickens. Remove from heat and gradually whisk in butter, until smooth. Stir in vanilla extract.

• • • • •

The beauty of this versatile dessert is that almost any bread imaginable can be used to make it. Brioche, pannetone, challah, croissants, raisin bread—even doughnuts, stale or otherwise, can be used as the basis for a rich, delicious pudding.

{ SOCIABLE SETTINGS }

The formal dinner table is one that requires care—from the time it takes to iron fine linens to the prim placement of silver forks, knives, and spoons. These occasions, however, are among the most special, making all the extra time and attention well worth the effort, particularly when your most precious pieces are used to create a stunning table.

THE GUEST LIST

The guests at your table should be selected and placed as carefully as the china. For obvious reasons, those with similar interests will have more to talk about as they dine. When devising the seating arrangement, try to place guests close to each other who you feel may have the most in common—be it two literature lovers or a single man and woman. This will ensure lively conversation!

A FORMAL AFFAIR

In my office, sitting on a bookshelf at eye-level, is Lillian Eichler's 1940 edition of *The New Book of Etiquette*. The pages are yellowing and the dust jacket is becoming more frayed about the edges with each passing year, so I handle this treasured tome carefully when thumbing through it, which I do frequently. Though written before I was born, I have to agree with Miss Lillian when she says "times change, manners improve."

The intricate etiquette of more formal entertaining has indeed changed over time. I recall sitting down with Grandmother Hoffman soon after my marriage and sorting through her heirloom silverware collection. I marveled not only at the generations of the Hoffman family that were represented in that collection, but also at the lovely pieces that were no longer commonly found at the formal table—fish forks and knives, even forks for ice cream. Today, a five-piece silver place setting is more than sufficient for most formal affairs. And as silverware and tablewares have evolved, so have the guidelines of etiquette. What was in vogue over 60 years ago in Lillian Eichler's day isn't necessarily a rigid rule for this generation. What has not changed, as Miss Lillian so wisely stated, is the importance of good manners, the "rules" of which have always been based on simple courtesy. Remember this and you will feel comfortable at any table, any time.

THE GUEST LIST

The guests at your table should be selected and placed as carefully as the china. For obvious reasons, those with similar interests will have more to talk about as they dine. When devising the seating arrangement, try to place guests close to each other who you feel may have the most in common—be it two literature lovers or a single man and woman. This will ensure lively conversation!

PROPER SETTING

To correctly set a formal table, first consider the arrangement. This is determined by the size of the table and the number of guests. A space of 16 to 20 inches should be allowed for each guest; this is called the "cover." The cover is marked by a centered service plate or charger. The napkin can be positioned on top of the plate, to the left of it, or even prettily presented in the water goblet—this is more dependant on the decorative design of the table than rules of etiquette.

The placement of silver at each cover is a bit more strict. Forks—never more than three at any one time—are placed to the left of the plate in the order of use. Spoons and knives are to the right, with the blades of the knives turned inward. The dessert spoon or fork can be placed at the top of the plate or simply served with the dessert.

The water goblet is placed directly above the tip of the knife, with a wine or tea glass to the right. The bread and butter plate is stationed above the tips of the forks, with the butter knife resting horizontally across the edge.

OPPOSITE: Hurricane globes nestled in sprays of berries, flowers, playful pumpkins, and tiny birds' nests filled with tealights—all lend an autumnesque feeling of abundance to the otherwise simple tablescape.

THE DECORATIVE TABLE

Though you want guests to have a comfortable space to dine, as long as accent and decorative pieces do not distract or detract from the dinner service, then, by all means, use them as abundantly as you like. Gilded fruit and tasseled napkin rings may have no practical purpose at a formal table, but they certainly add a patina of luster and polish. Another simple idea, and one that makes a sophisticated statement, is using tiny picture frames as place card holders. For an especially gracious touch, give the frames to your guests as keepsakes of the dinner.

COLOR SCHEMES

"In the silver, linen, and crystal of the dinner table one reads the story of the hostess's personality," Miss Lillian writes. "If she has excellent taste, her table tells it." This is indeed important advice to remember, not only when choosing dinnerware patterns or linens, but in seeing the whole picture.

The serving pieces and accessories in your wardrobe of tablewares should not only serve as an expression of your personal taste, but should also work in tandem with the colors in your dining room.

Needless to say, in setting the table for dinner—whether formal or informal—the silver must be well polished, the linen faultlessly laundered, the china and glassware sparkling.

—LILLIAN EICHLER

Because china is as ornamental to the table as a vase is to a mantle, choose colors that excite and inspire you!

A monochromatic tone-on-tone color scheme, for instance, is an elegant choice with timeless appeal, one that brings balance and interest to any room. Rather than using only a single hue, however, try wall colors and tablewares in different shades of the same tone. In the same vein, an analogous color scheme is subtle in look, but powerful in appeal. Analogous colors are neighbors on the color wheel—yellow and orange, blue and green, etc. For this kind of color scheme, consider choosing a paint for your walls that will serve as the primary shade; this will allow you to use different sets of china and accent pieces in harmonious secondary tones.

Another option is choosing china and wall colors that contrast—one warm, one cool. For instance, china and serving pieces in chocolate, cream, or biscuit can create a dynamic visual contrast in a dining room painted in a number of colors, from a spicy pumpkin to a deep teal.

OPPOSITE: Notice how sparingly color is used in the table accessories. Only in the pears is the wall color echoed.

IMPECCABLE SERVICE

No matter how lovely the table, a dinner that isn't properly served will be considered less than a stellar success. As few of us are lucky enough to be attended to by a staff of trained servers, it pays for the well-heeled hostess to understand the basics of *service à la russe*.

This classic style of sequentially served courses often starts with soup, which is served from the left with the left hand. As this course

OPPOSITE: Because chargers are not included in most five-piece services, choose one that complements your formal china pattern, and preferably one that will mix and match with numerous styles.

ends, the soup bowl is cleared from the right and replaced from the left with the plate for the next course—salad and so on. Dishes are removed singly, never stacked.

As the primary courses are eaten—soup, fish, entrée, and salad—wine, water, or tea goblets should be refilled as needed, without moving the glasses. It is customary to brush crumbs from the table before dessert is served; salt and pepper shakers or salt cellars should also be removed at this time.

I have many salt cellars in my own collection, and I love to see these ornamental pieces returning to formal tables. At one time, when salt was still a pricy imported product, salt cellars were also used to declare status and a sort of pecking order at the dining table. The most distinguished guests were asked to sit between the hostess and the salt cellar. These guests were considered "above the salt."

ABOVE RIGHT: Some salt cellars are lidded, to protect the salt from moisture. These dainty dishes are also sometimes referred to as salt dips, or if lidless, open salts.

HOLIDAY DINNER

THE MEMBERS OF YOUR FAMILY SHOULD ALWAYS BE TREATED AS HONORED GUESTS AT YOUR TABLE, ESPECIALLY FOR A FORMAL THANKSGIVING OR CHRISTMAS DINNER.

When we think of formal entertaining, we don't often include our own families in the list of guests who deserve special care at our table. And certainly, the sometimes less relaxed rules of formal dining are not in keeping with the family dinner hour, a time when we can unwind in the company of those we love most and enjoy a comfortable meal together. However, there is something to be said for occasionally bringing out your best china, crystal, and manners for family, and there is no more appropriate time to do so than during the holiday season.

In fact, as Miss Lillian points out, "the one way to achieve poise or assurance is to practice dining in private as in public, so that the correct thing becomes instinctive rather than studied." Absolutely true. When dining formally with family, especially children and young adults, don't miss the opportunity to teach your young relatives the finer points of dinner table etiquette and to hone your own skills.

Tip: This delicious relish—accented by the crunch of pecans and sweetened by the delicate flavors of orange and honey—is wonderful with roast turkey, ham, or chicken. Leftovers will keep for at least a week, and are delicious served on turkey sandwiches.

ROASTED TURKEY WITH GARLIC LEMON BUTTER
Yield: 8 to 10 servings

1   cup butter, room temperature
2   tablespoons chopped fresh garlic
2   tablespoons fresh lemon juice
1½ teaspoons salt
1   teaspoon ground black pepper
1   (16 to 18-pound) whole turkey
Garnish: fresh rosemary sprigs, fresh thyme sprigs

1. Preheat oven to 325°.
2. In a medium bowl, combine butter, garlic, lemon juice, salt, and pepper. Rub butter mixture on skin and in cavity of turkey. Truss turkey with butcher's twine. Place turkey, breast-side up, on a rack in a roasting pan. Cover with foil and bake 3 hours.
3. Remove foil and continue baking 1 hour, or until meat thermometer inserted into the thigh reaches 180°. Baste turkey with pan juices periodically. Remove turkey from oven and let rest for 10 minutes. Garnish with fresh rosemary and thyme sprigs, if desired. Serve with pan juices.

CRANBERRY RELISH
Yield: 8 to 10 servings

1¼ cups sugar
½   cup water
½   cup fresh orange juice
2   tablespoons orange zest
1   (12-ounce) package fresh cranberries
½   cup finely chopped pecans
1   tablespoon honey
Garnish: orange zest strips

1. In a medium saucepan over medium-high heat, combine sugar, water, orange juice, and orange zest; stir to dissolve sugar. Bring to a boil; add cranberries. Return to a boil, reduce heat, simmer 10 minutes stirring occasionally.
2. Remove from heat and add pecans and honey, stirring to combine. Cool slightly; cover and chill. Garnish with orange zest strips, if desired.

Tip: No holiday plate in the South would be complete without a serving of cornbread dressing. For an extra rich flavor, we've added another Southern classic to the list of ingredients— crumbled cooked biscuits. What a wonderful use for surplus breakfast biscuits!

CORNBREAD DRESSING
Yield: 10 to 12 servings

2   (6-ounce) packages buttermilk cornbread mix
½   cup butter
2   cups chopped onion
2   cups chopped celery
2   cups crumbled cooked biscuits, homemade or frozen
1   tablespoon poultry seasoning
1   teaspoon salt
½   teaspoon ground black pepper
4½ cups chicken broth
1   (10.75-ounce) can cream of chicken soup
3   large eggs, lightly beaten

1. Prepare and bake cornbread mix according to package directions. Cool, and crumble; set aside. Preheat oven to 350°. Lightly grease 13x9x2-inch baking dish.
2. In a large skillet, melt butter over medium-high heat. Add onion and celery; cook, stirring constantly, for 7 minutes, or until tender.
3. In a large bowl, combine crumbled cornbread, crumbled biscuits, poultry seasoning, salt, and pepper; stir in vegetable mixture. Add broth, soup, and eggs, stirring well. Pour mixture into prepared baking dish. Bake 45 to 50 minutes, or until center is set.

CREAMED ENGLISH PEAS
Yield: 8 to 10 servings

4   cups water
1   (10-ounce) bag pearl onions, peeled
1½ teaspoons salt
2   (16-ounce) packages frozen green peas
1   red bell pepper, chopped
¼   cup butter
2   tablespoons all-purpose flour
1   teaspoon sugar
½   teaspoon salt
¼   teaspoon ground black pepper
¼   teaspoon ground nutmeg
1   cup heavy cream

{ RECIPE CONTINUES ON PAGE 126 }

Tip. For a gracious touch at the formal table, try my trick. Soften several sticks of butter to room temperature and smooth into the candy molds of your choice. Freeze the molds until the butter is firm, and serve to your guests with rolls. Just remember to keep the butter molds cold until you're ready to serve dinner.

1. In a large saucepan, combine water, onions, and salt over medium-high heat. Bring to a boil and cook 5 minutes. Add peas and bell pepper and cook 5 minutes, or until peas are just tender. Drain vegetables and set aside, reserving ¾ cup cooking liquid.

2. In a large saucepan, melt butter over medium heat. Add flour, sugar, salt, pepper, and nutmeg, stirring constantly for 3 minutes. Gradually add reserved liquid, whisking until smooth. Add cream, and cook, whisking constantly, until thickened. Add vegetables and cook 1 minute, or until heated through.

ROAST HARVEST MEDLEY
Yield: 8 to 10 servings

6   medium beets, peeled and cut into ½-inch cubes
4   large carrots, peeled and sliced to ½-inch thickness
4   large parsnips, peeled and sliced to ½-inch thickness
1   acorn squash, peeled, seeded, and cut into ½-inch cubes
2   large sweet potatoes, peeled and cut into ½-inch cubes
¼   cup olive oil
1   tablespoon chopped fresh thyme
1   tablespoon chopped fresh rosemary
1½ teaspoons salt
½   teaspoon ground black pepper

1. Preheat oven to 450°. Line a shallow roasting pan with aluminum foil; set aside.

2. In a large bowl combine beets, carrots, parsnips, squash and sweet potatoes. In a small bowl, combine olive oil, thyme, rosemary, salt, and pepper. Combine vegetables and olive oil mixture, tossing to coat evenly. Bake 45 to 50 minutes, or until tender, gently stirring half-way through cooking time.

• • • • •

Not only practical in purpose, covered vegetable dishes are also a lovely addition to the dinner table. These, along with platters, gravy boats, sauce boats, and soup tureens are servingwares that should be included in the china sets you collect.

Tip. Lumps in your mashed potatoes are fine, but not in your giblet gravy! For satiny-smooth gravy, make sure the butter and flour are hot and the chicken broth is at room temperature before combining. If the broth is warm or hot, it will cause the glutens in the flour to seize and create lumps.

CLASSIC MASHED POTATOES
Yield: 8 to 10 servings

4   pounds Idaho potatoes, peeled and cut into 1-inch pieces
2   cups heavy cream, warmed and divided
1/2 cup butter, softened
Salt to taste
Ground black pepper to taste
Garnish: chopped fresh parsley

1. Place potatoes in a Dutch oven with enough salted water to cover. Bring to a boil over medium heat; cook for approximately 15 minutes, or until potatoes are tender. Turn off burner, drain potatoes completely, and return to stove.
2. Mash potatoes with a potato masher. Add 1½ cups cream and butter, stirring until butter is melted. If smoother texture is desired, beat with an electric mixer at medium speed until potatoes reach a smooth consistency, adding additional ½ cup cream if needed. Season with salt and pepper to taste. Garnish with chopped fresh parsley, if desired.

GIBLET GRAVY
Yield: 5 cups

1/4 cup butter
1/4 cup all-purpose flour
4   cups chicken broth
1   (10.5-ounce) can cream of chicken soup
1/2 teaspoon salt
1/4 teaspoon ground black pepper
2   hard-boiled eggs, chopped
Turkey giblets, cooked and chopped

1. In a medium saucepan, melt butter over medium heat. Whisk in flour; cook 5 minutes, whisking constantly. Gradually add chicken broth, whisking constantly until smooth.
2. Add soup, salt, and pepper, whisking until smooth. Add eggs and giblets, stirring to combine. Reduce heat to low and simmer 10 minutes, stirring frequently.

CHRISTENING PARTY

SERVED FOLLOWING THE CHURCH SERVICE, A CHRISTENING LUNCHEON
IS A WONDERFUL OPPORTUNITY TO CELEBRATE WITH A BEAUTIFUL
TABLE AND A SUMPTUOUS MEAL.

A formal luncheon following the church christening of an infant is a joyous occasion, and one that is worthy of a formally set table. Soft, baby-fresh tones at the table punctuated by bright pops of color create a tablescape that is simply enchanting, and in keeping with the spirit of such a blessed event. It's also a wonderful idea to tailor the color scheme to the gender of the child—blues for boys and fresh pinks for girls. For the luncheon, the food should be elegant yet filling, and if possible, with a menu of dishes that can be prepared prior to the church service.

TOP: While also beautiful, the flowers used on this table were also chosen for their symbolic meaning. Tulips signify perfect love—the color white symbolizes innocence and purity.

Tip. Chicken with Basil Cream and Angel Hair Pasta is light and elegant, yet satisfying enough for even the heartiest appetite. If you have trouble finding the prosciutto that is called for in the recipe, simply substitute Virginia country ham or even bacon.

CHICKEN WITH BASIL CREAM AND ANGEL HAIR PASTA

Yield: 8 servings

¼ cup extra virgin olive oil
4 pounds boneless, skinless chicken breasts, cut into ½-inch strips
½ teaspoon freshly ground black pepper
1 cup chopped prosciutto
1 tablespoon minced garlic
4 cups heavy cream
1½ cups shredded Parmesan cheese
1 cup thinly sliced fresh basil
¼ teaspoon salt
1 (1-pound) package angel hair pasta, cooked
Garnish: shredded Parmesan cheese

1. In a 12-inch nonstick skillet over medium-high heat, heat olive oil. Season chicken with pepper, and cook, stirring constantly for 15 minutes, or until lightly browned. Remove chicken, leaving as much oil in pan as possible; set aside.
2. Add prosciutto and garlic; cook, stirring constantly for 2 minutes. Add cream, cheese, basil, and salt. Bring to a simmer, stirring until the cheese is melted.
3. Add cooked chicken; reduce heat to low, and simmer approximately 15 minutes, or until chicken is tender. Serve with angel hair pasta. Garnish with Parmesan cheese, if desired.

• • • • •

The beauty of this entrée is that much of the work can be done before the church service. For the Chicken with Basil Cream and Angel Hair Pasta, complete step one before leaving for church, then prepare the sauce and pasta while guests are arriving—the dish will go from kitchen to table in less than 30 minutes flat.

Tip. For perfect vegetable ribbons, trim the sides of the vegetables to a square shape before shaving with a vegetable peeler. Also, be sure and choose yellow squash that is long and thin in shape.

134

VEGETABLE RIBBONS
Yield: 8 servings

6   large carrots, peeled
4   large zucchini squash
4   large yellow squash
6   tablespoons butter, divided
¼   cup extra virgin olive oil, divided
2   tablespoon fresh thyme leaves, divided
½   teaspoon salt, divided
½   teaspoon ground black pepper, divided

1. In a medium bowl, cut thin ribbons of carrots, zucchini, and squash with a vegetable peeler; set aside.
2. In a large sauté pan over medium-high heat, heat 3 tablespoons butter and 2 tablespoons oil until melted. Add half of the vegetables and cook, stirring constantly for approximately 5 minutes, or until vegetables are tender. Stir in 1 tablespoon thyme, ¼ teaspoon salt, and ¼ teaspoon pepper and cook 1 minute. Remove to serving bowl and keep warm.
3. Repeat procedure with remaining ingredients. Serve immediately.

GARLIC CRESCENTS
Yield: 16 crescents

½   cup butter, softened
1   tablespoon grated Parmesan cheese
1   tablespoon chopped fresh parsley
½   teaspoon garlic powder
2   (8-ounce) cans refrigerated crescent rolls

1. Preheat oven to 375°. Line a baking sheet with parchment paper.
2. In a small bowl, combine butter, cheese, parsley, and garlic powder.
3. Unroll dough and separate along perforations into 16 triangles. Spread about ½ teaspoon butter mixture over triangles and roll into crescents, following package directions.
4. Place on prepared baking sheet. Bake 10 to 12 minutes, or until golden brown. Additional butter mixture may be melted and brushed on warm rolls, if desired.

Tip: A nice change from a plain Jane tossed salad, Broccoli Salad Vinaigrette can be prepared a day in advance of the lunch—just leave out the mush-rooms and feta, and add both just before serving.

BROCCOLI SALAD VINAIGRETTE
Yield: 8 servings

4	cups fresh broccoli florets
3	cups fresh cauliflower florets
1	(8-ounce) container sliced fresh mushrooms
2	cups halved grape tomatoes
1	cup chopped green olives
1	shallot, minced
1/2	cup olive oil
1/2	cup red wine vinegar
2	tablespoons sugar
2	teaspoons Italian seasoning
2	teaspoons Dijon mustard
1	clove garlic, minced
1/2	cup crumbled feta cheese

1. In a large bowl, combine broccoli, cauliflower, mushrooms, tomatoes, olives, and shallot; set aside.

2. In a small bowl, whisk together olive oil, vinegar, sugar, Italian seasoning, mustard, and garlic. Pour oil mixture over broccoli mixture, tossing to combine. Cover and chill 2 to 4 hours. Sprinkle feta cheese over salad before serving.

• • • • •

If some of the ingredients in the Broccoli Salad Vinaigrette aren't to your taste, don't be afraid to experiment with substitutions—a vinaigrette-based salad is very adaptable to other flavors. For instance, leave out the olives, mushrooms, Italian seasoning and Dijon mustard; use Balsamic vinegar instead of the red wine version, and add dried cranberries and roasted pecans or walnuts. The possibilities are endless—especially with the variety of flavored vinegars now commonly available in grocery stores.

Tip. If peaches are in season, use them in place of fresh strawberries. To convert the recipe, use Peach Schnapps in place of strawberry extract and syrup, and peach jelly instead of strawberry.

STRAWBERRY CHARLOTTE
Yield: 1 (8¹/₂-inch) Charlotte

2 (3-ounce) packages ladyfingers, split
¹/₄ cup cold water
1 envelope unflavored gelatin
1 (8-ounce) package cream cheese, softened
¹/₄ cup unsalted butter, softened
¹/₄ cup strawberry syrup
2 teaspoons strawberry extract
1 cup confectioners' sugar
2 cups heavy cream
1 tablespoon sugar
1 (1-pound) container fresh strawberries, divided
¹/₄ cup strawberry jelly, melted

1. Line bottom of (8¹/₂-inch) springform pan with waxed paper. Lightly spray the bottom and sides with cooking spray. Line the bottom and sides of the pan with ladyfingers, making sure they fit together snugly.
2. In a small microwave-safe bowl, combine water and gelatin; let stand 5 minutes. Microwave on High (100 percent power) in 30-second intervals until dissolved (approximately 1 minute total); cool slightly.
3. In a medium bowl, combine cream cheese, butter, strawberry syrup, and strawberry extract. Beat at medium speed with an electric mixer until creamy. Gradually add confectioners' sugar, mixing well; set aside.
4. In a separate bowl, beat cream and sugar at high speed, until soft peaks form. Beat in dissolved gelatin until stiff peaks form. Fold together the cream cheese mixture and the whipped cream mixture until well combined.
5. To assemble, evenly spread half of the cream mixture over ladyfingers in bottom of pan. Place an even layer of sliced strawberries on top of cream mixture. Spoon other half of cream mixture over strawberries. Cover with plastic wrap and chill for 4 hours.
6. To serve, remove plastic wrap and run a knife around the edge of the pan. Carefully unlatch ring of springform pan and unmold. Arrange remaining sliced strawberries on top of cream mixture. Brush strawberries with melted strawberry jelly.

{ NEIGHBORLY GET-TOGETHERS }

Thoreau wrote that "one is wise to cultivate the tree that bears fruit in our soul." So too, our neighbors. Those people who live to our left and to our right, three doors down and two streets over; who offer their friendship and a cup of sugar when we're without; whose children grow into adults with our own—these are friendships worth cultivating. A special get-together just for our neighbors is not only reason to set a sumptuous table, but also to celebrate the people who share in the milestone moments of our lives.

FEAST FOR FRIENDS

Every year in January, I invite a group of girls from the neighborhood to join me for a little post-Christmas gathering. To pay penance for all the cookies, cakes, and candies we exchanged and devoured over the holidays, I serve a feast of fresh fruit in my finest silver. The dressed-up diet party is a wonderful way to enjoy each other's company and help us stick to those New Year's resolutions!

CLUB MEETING

FORMING NEIGHBORHOOD SOCIAL CLUBS IS A GREAT WAY TO EXPLORE COMMON INTERESTS AND MAKE NEW FRIENDS.

One of my dearest friends was my neighbor even before she was my friend. Barbara Cockerham and her husband Jim lived next door when my husband Wayne and I were newlyweds. We have been the best of friends ever since. In the early years, one of our greatest mutual interests was needlework—a hobby that eventually led Barbara and me to publish magazines together. It was she who taught me the art of cross-stitching, and we formed a stitching circle with other friends and neighbors. Many a lovely lunch was shared with these wonderful women, taking turns entertaining each other in our homes, stitching, chatting, and simply getting to know one another.

Whether it's needlework, books, or a sewing circle that draws you together, forming a neighborhood social club is a fabulous way to deepen and explore your personal interests, relax, and get to know the people in your immediate community. Whether you meet in the afternoon for lunch or after work for dinner, when it's your turn to host the event, take pains to set the scene with flair.

I see heaven's glories shine and faith shines equal.
—EMILY BRONTË

Try theming the menu and table design to suit the occasion. For a garden club meeting, that might be afternoon tea with a table set with spring flowers and Shelley chintz china. For a book club meeting, consider the material to be discussed. If your group is reading Emily Brontë, tablewares with English manor appeal are just the thing. Accent the look with ornate cut-crystal goblets, footed tidbit dishes, and other Victorian-style serving pieces. An antique cruet set, for instance, is indicative of the Victorian period, and is a wonderful conversation piece that hearkens to the spirit of the event and to the era of author.

OPPOSITE: Vintage cruet sets contain stoppered glass bottles for liquid condiments, such as vinegar, oil, and lemon juice, as well as salt and pepper holders, and sometimes a mustard pot or muffineer. Sometimes called a sugar caster, a muffineer has a pierced lid and is filled with sugar and sometimes cinnamon for dusting hot buttered bread and muffins.

WELCOMING NEW NEIGHBORS

A TABLE SET WITH COUNTRY FRESH DINNERWARES AND SERVING PIECES IS AN INVITATION TO SIT, SUP, AND SOCIALIZE.

Being the new family on the block can be overwhelming, and simple courtesy demands that we welcome new neighbors into the fold with sincerity and warmth. In fact, the great arbiter of etiquette, Emily Post, says that when strangers move into the community, "it is not only unfriendly, but uncivil for their neighbors not to call on them."

I agree with Emily Post, and I have always made it a point to seek out neighborhood newcomers. On moving day, I like to greet families with a smile and a bit of hospitality to help ease the stress of getting settled. Perhaps a hot supper of homemade soup and cornbread would be appreciated on moving night, or better still, a pound of freshly ground coffee, juice, sticky buns, and fruit for breakfast the next morning. I add a card with important information—my own phone number, reliable vendors, directions to a nearby supermarket, phone numbers for trusted babysitters, etc.—and a handwritten note of welcome that includes an invitation to lunch or dinner once all the boxes are unpacked.

For these get-togethers, you may or may not wish to invite other neighbors as well, but do keep the tone casual. An extravagant dinner served on formal china might be off-putting, so keep it light. A table set with country crockery,

on the other hand, is more approachably attractive. The rich colors and homespun charm that characterize the farmhouse country style makes this design scheme ideal for a lunch or dinner with new neighbors—stylish, but not over-the-top.

Of course, you'll want to offer your new neighbors a housewarming gift. A potted plant, a sterling silver picture frame, or a crystal bud vase are always lovely options. A casserole dish from the china pattern in which your entrée is served is even more special, and will remind your neighbors of your thoughtfulness every time they see it or use it for a dinner in their own home.

ABOVE: Though it looks like a vintage piece, this covered bowl is the epitome of country chic. Animal and vegetable motifs are traditional symbols of graciousness.

NEIGHBORHOOD BREAKFAST

Summertime is the right time for entertaining neighbors, but in the South, the temperatures can soar even before lunch. Why not beat the heat by inviting over a few neighbors for a patio or poolside breakfast? While the kids splash around in the pool or play in the back yard, moms and dads can kick back and enjoy a little time together without languishing in the summer heat and humidity. For such an outdoor table, try china in summery hues, simple cotton linens with floral-themed napkin rings that mimic summer blooms, and a modest centerpiece of fresh-cut flowers or greenery.

{ GRAND GET-TOGETHERS }

During vacation season when the weather is divine, kids are out of school, and families are in between holidays and other obligations, the timing couldn't be better for a grand get-together with all the neighbors. Try these tips to organize an old-fashioned block party:

- Start organizing the block party two to three months in advance. Depending on the size of your neighborhood, you'll need a different team or person in charge of invitations, equipment, refreshments, entertainment, activities, set-up and clean-up, and decorations.

- Make sure everyone is invited to the party—no exceptions here—and ask for an RSVP. Also, be sure and note a "rain date" on invitations.

- Assign someone to liaison with the neighborhood association (if there is one) as well as city hall and the police department. Permission and permits may be required from each, and police will often provide barricades to block streets off for the party. Insurance may also be required—find out.

- Decide how you want to handle food—this will depend on your neighbors. A potluck may be everyone's choice, or if you have willing and able cooks, grilled fare for all might be the best option. In this case, ask for a donation during the party to recoup costs or consider asking each invited family for a small fee beforehand to cover the cost of food and beverages.

- Make sure activities are planned for all age groups, from games for pre-schoolers to something of interest for teenagers and adults.

- Consider contacting local businesses such as bakeries, gift shops, and others for donated door prizes to give away during the party. Make sure the merchants' business names are announced as prizes are handed out—a little free publicity is a great incentive to give.

- Provide plenty of trash receptacles and place them strategically around the perimeter of the party—this will help alleviate much of the after-party clean up.

Better is a neighbor that is near than a brother far off.
—PROVERBS 27:10

IMPROMPTU PICNIC

A MENU OF SOUTHERN FAVORITES WILL PLEASE EVERY PALATE AT A SUMMER PICNIC FOR NEIGHBORS AND FRIENDS.

There's nothing more neighborly than a picnic, and even if it's raining, don't be afraid to break out the hamper and call a few neighbors over for a little back-porch fun. A few pillows, blankets, baskets, darling tablewares, good food, and you'll be serving up your own brand of sunshine in no time.

OPPOSITE: If you have plenty of baskets lying around the house, put them to good use. Wicker and woven baskets make pretty work of transporting china, linens, food, and more to your picnic.

Tip: Though I usually use juice only, our recipe for Watermelon Lemonade calls for a bit of melon liqueur to heighten the melon taste. If children or non-drinkers are invited, simply skip that ingredient.

WATERMELON LEMONADE
Yield: 1 gallon

3   cups cubed, seeded watermelon
1   (12-ounce) can frozen pink lemonade concentrate, thawed
¾   cup melon liqueur
3½ cups cold water
Garnish: lemon slices

1. Place watermelon in the work bowl of an electric blender or food processor; process until smooth.
2. Combine watermelon puree, lemonade concentrate, melon liqueur, and water in a pitcher; stir well. Garnish each glass with lemon slice, if desired.

LEMON-BASIL PASTA SALAD
Yield: 8 servings

1   (8-ounce) package bowtie pasta, cooked
2   cups broccoli florets
2   cups sliced carrots
2   cups sliced mushrooms
2   (2.25-ounce) can sliced black olives, drained
¼   cup capers, drained
1   recipe Lemon-Basil Vinaigrette (recipe follows)

1. Cook pasta according to package directions; drain, and set aside.
2. In a large saucepan, blanch broccoli and carrots in boiling water over high heat for 1 minute. Drain broccoli and carrots, and rinse immediately in cold water to stop the cooking process.
3. In a large bowl, combine broccoli, carrots, mushrooms, black olives, and capers. Add pasta tossing gently to combine. Add Lemon-Basil Vinaigrette; toss well. Cover and chill.

• • • • •

Don't just eat your veggies—use them to enhance the presentation of your picnic. A bowl lined with red cabbage leaves is perfect for the pasta salad while bell peppers are naturally colorful containers for dip.

Tip: Leftover pasta salad? Don't throw it out! Add a bit of crabmeat, steamed shrimp, or cooked chicken and you have a wonderful lunch or dinner in a jiffy.

LEMON-BASIL VINAIGRETTE
Yield: approximately ³/₄ cup

2   tablespoons fresh basil, chopped
2   tablespoons lemon zest
¹/₂ teaspoon kosher salt
¹/₂ teaspoon garlic salt
¹/₈ teaspoon ground white pepper
¹/₂ cup extra virgin olive oil
4   tablespoons lemon juice
2   tablespoons white wine vinegar
2   tablespoons whole grain mustard

In a lidded jar, combine all ingredients, cover tightly, and shake vigorously.

TRIPLE PEPPER AND BACON DIP
Yield: about 3 cups

2   cups sour cream
1   (3-ounce) package cream cheese, softened
1   cup finely shredded Mexican four-cheese blend
³/₄ cup salsa
¹/₄ cup finely chopped red bell pepper
¹/₄ cup finely chopped green bell pepper
¹/₄ cup finely chopped yellow bell pepper
¹/₄ cup minced green onion
2   (3-ounce) packages real bacon bits or pieces
¹/₂ teaspoon chili powder
¹/₄ teaspoon garlic salt

In a large bowl, add all ingredients, stirring to combine. Cover and chill. Serve with assorted fresh vegetables.

Tip. If you have the time, marinate chicken pieces overnight in buttermilk rather than chicken broth and white Worcestershire. Buttermilk, which has acidic properties, tenderizes the chicken and improves the flavor.

FRIED CHICKEN
Yield: 4-6 servings

2   quarts chicken broth
1   cup white Worcestershire sauce
1   (3½ to 4-pound) chicken cut into 8 or 9 pieces or 3 pounds chicken pieces
2   cups all-purpose flour
2   teaspoons salt
2   teaspoons ground white pepper
1   cup buttermilk
½   cup or more canola oil or other vegetable oil (for frying)

1. In a large bowl, combine broth and Worcestershire sauce. Add chicken and marinate for 1 hour, covered, in refrigerator. Drain chicken and pat dry with paper towels.
2. In a shallow bowl or pie plate, combine flour, salt, and pepper.
3. In a medium bowl, place buttermilk.
4. Dredge each chicken piece in flour mixture, dip in buttermilk, and dredge in flour mixture again. Set aside.
5. In a large heavy skillet (preferably cast iron), pour ½-inch oil and heat to 325° over medium-high heat. Add chicken, skin-side down, beginning with dark meat pieces. Keeping oil temperature between 325° and 350°, fry chicken on each side for 5 to 6 minutes covered, and then 5 to 6 minutes uncovered, turning twice. Total cooking time should be 20 to 24 minutes. (Chicken is done when a thermometer inserted in thickest part registers 165°). Drain chicken on a wire rack.

DREAMPIES
Yield: about 1 dozen cookies

1   cup unsalted butter, softened
1½ cups sugar
1   teaspoon vanilla extract
4   large egg yolks
2½ cups all-purpose flour
⅔   cup unsweetened cocoa
½   teaspoon salt
Marshmallows (recipe follows)
2   (16-ounce) packages chocolate candy coating, melted

{ RECIPE CONTINUES ON PAGE 164 }

Tip: The combination of chocolate, graham crackers, and fluffy marshmallow is said to have started as a commercial cookie made special for Southern coal miners around the turn of the twentieth century. Our version uses a chocolate cookie and homemade marshmallows.

1. Preheat oven to 325°. Lightly grease 2 baking sheets with nonstick cooking spray.

2. In a large bowl using an electric mixer, beat butter and sugar on high until creamy. Add vanilla extract and mix to combine. Add egg yolks one at a time, mixing well after each addition.

3. In a large bowl, sift together flour, cocoa, and salt. Slowly add flour mixture to butter mixture until combined.

4. Form dough into a 6-inch disc and wrap with plastic wrap. Chill for 1 hour.

5. On a lightly floured surface, roll dough to ¼-inch thickness. Using a 3½-inch round cutter, cut dough into 12 rounds and place on baking sheets.

6. Bake 6 minutes. Let cool on pan 1 minute. Remove and cool completely on wire rack.

7. Cut marshmallows with 3½-inch round cutter. Sandwich between 2 chocolate cookies. Place on wire rack positioned over parchment paper.

8. Pour melted chocolate over cookies and allow to set.

MARSHMALLOWS
Yield: 1 dozen 3½-inch round marshmallows

3½ envelopes gelatin
1   cup water, divided
2   cups sugar
½   cup light corn syrup
2   large egg whites
1   teaspoon vanilla extract
¼   teaspoon salt
¼   cup confectioners' sugar

1. Lightly spray a jellyroll pan with nonstick cooking spray (with flour); set aside.

2. In a medium bowl, stir together gelatin with ½ cup water; set aside.

3. In a small saucepan, cook sugar, corn syrup, and ½ cup water over medium-high heat, stirring constantly, until sugar is dissolved. Cook, without stirring, until mixture reaches 240° on a candy thermometer.

4. With an electric mixer, beat egg whites with vanilla extract and salt at high speed until stiff peaks form.

5. Add hot syrup mixture to gelatin mixture and beat on high speed with electric mixer until mixture is thick and tripled in volume (about 4 minutes).

6. Fold in egg whites.

7. Pour mixture in jelly roll pan and evenly spread. Sprinkle with confectioners' sugar to cover. Chill in refrigerator 2 hours, or until set.

{ POLITE CONVERSATION }

In today's hustle-bustle world, so much it seems, is lost in translation. No doubt cell phones, e-mails, and instant-message missives have made communication more expedient, but what we have perhaps sacrificed in the name of quicker, faster, and better is simple heart-to-heart conversation. Setting the scene for such moments is not only a worthy endeavor, but, I believe, as restorative as a tonic.

A GARDEN VISTA

SETTING THE STAGE FOR EASY FLOW OF CONVERSATION BETWEEN YOU AND YOUR GUESTS STARTS WITH A BEAUTIFUL VIEW.

When we leave the hectic world behind, entering a setting such as this one, we want it to be a departure that leaves us speechless. Why? Because that's exactly the kind of stimulus we need to uncork the flow of conversation. After all, even the most outgoing among us can be at least a little shy when we are first seated at the table. To help spark some banter, begin a bit more naturally, give your guests something besides each other to talk about—and to look at.

Setting your table with a deliberate eye to the surrounding view helps ensure effortless dialogue. When weather and conditions permit, nothing accomplishes this task more easily than creating an airy vista in the glorious outdoors. Surrounded by the lushness of nature's bounty, who can resist commenting on the verdant hues of garden flowers, their heady scent, and the sunny skies above?

A table set with china, linens, blooms, and greenery that mimic Mother Nature's bounty adds both to the effect and the occasion. I like to dress up simple patio furniture with exquisite, handmade linens, such as a Battenburg lace tablecloth. Table and glasswares that are subtle in design and hue seem at home in the al fresco setting, while adding a bit of formal flair to the table.

AFTERNOON TEA

Though it is often viewed—unfairly I think—as a stodgy affair, afternoon tea is not only a delightful escape from the stresses of the day, but is also a perfect time to catch up in conversation with those you care for; tea slows us down by creating a moment of contentment. Serving tea at an outdoor table lessens the sense of formality while enhancing the feeling of intimacy—an integral part of what makes afternoon tea such a simple pleasure.

RIGHT: The "shabby chic" appeal of weather-worn patio furniture paired with bone china and pristine linens is a delicious contrast for afternoon tea service. Simple greenery and flowers from the garden provide perfect table accents.

Conversation ... is the art of never appearing a bore, of knowing how to say everything interestingly, to entertain with no matter what, to be charming with nothing at all.

—GUY DE MAUPASSANT

There are many rules of etiquette at the tea table. Milk is added last, not first; tea is sipped not slurped; and a raised pinkie is not only unacceptable, it is a beacon of ineptitude. As foreboding as those rules may sound, however, such gaffes are forgivable—at least once. The kind of break from decorum you will no doubt be remembered for, however, is the introduction into the conversation topics that are verboten at the tea table because they are either in poor taste or not in keeping with the occasion. These include personal maladies, a dislike for the beverage or food that is being served, or malicious gossip. When joining others for afternoon tea, confine yourself to more pleasant discourse. Acceptable subjects of discussion include travel, books, the theatre, music, or other cultural pursuits and personal interests.

OPPOSITE: The creamer from your tea set makes a lovely impromptu vase for freshly cut garden flowers, adding to the visual interest of the table.

TABLE FOR TWO

EASY EXCHANGES WITH FAMILY, GIRLISH GOSSIP WITH FRIENDS, OR
A ROMANTIC DINNER Á DEUX—A BEAUTIFUL TABLE FOR TWO SETS
THE STAGE FOR INSTANT INTIMACY AND FRIENDLY FAMILIARITY.

Be it a sunrise breakfast with my daughter-in-law, midday soup and salad with a dear friend, or an early evening dinner with my husband, a table for two gives way to the kind of unhurried tête-à-tête we are so often robbed of in the daily pressures of life. And what's more, a scaled-down dining table set up on the patio, in the garden, or even indoors is a wonderful opportunity to make use of orphaned place settings snapped up at flea markets, antique stores, and jumble sales. In fact, I consciously collect single and dual place settings for just such occasions. Pulling it together in no time flat? A piece of cake.

Start with staging. The dinner table is wonderful for every day, but this is a special occasion! Make an instant impression by choosing an area of the home that is restful and secluded—such as a covered back porch. Patio furniture tucked away in a cozy nook is instantly elegant with the addition of gorgeous hand-embroidered linens covering the table and plump pillows on chairs. Next, add fresh flowers and dinnerware for two, so that all you need do is seat, serve, and enjoy!

OPPOSITE: Notice how the dinnerware, serving pieces, linens, and flower vase subtly complement the Victorianesque dinner platters that hang above the table. This helps complete the look and creates a palpable ambience.

174

As colors go, red packs a powerful punch. Its emotional intensity and rich saturation of hue never fails to get noticed. A little, however, can go a long way. For this particular tablescape, the table cloth and matching linens are creamy white with popping bursts of red that underscore the beauty of rosy-toned transferware serving plates, coffee cups and saucers. Flowers in deep magenta and pink add contrast and a deeper tonality of color to the overall affect.

OPPOSITE: The floral theme that pulls the tablescape together visually is echoed in the china, the linens, the etched crystal—even in the design of the silverware.

QUIET MOMENTS

CREATING A CONVERSATION-FRIENDLY TABLE FOR TWO REQUIRES A
HEALTHY DOSE OF IMAGINATION AND A SENSE OF SEATING AND SPACE.

Afternoon tea with your closest girlfriend is always worthy of your finest china, your freshest infusion of tea, and naturally, a resplendent table. But be creative. Instead of setting up your service at the dining room table, try something different. A window table in the living room, den, or parlor becomes a lovely seating area when arranged with comfortable high-backed upholstered chairs and adorned with the accoutrements of tea.

OPPOSITE: Notice the placement of the chairs in this seating arrangement. Their proximity promotes ease of conversation and serving. The chairs are set at a comfortable angle, creating a warm one-on-one space for tea and secrets shared.

*Ideal conversation must be an exchange of thought,
and not, as many of those who worry most about their shortcomings
believe, an eloquent exhibition of wit or oratory.*

—EMILY POST

When it comes to devising a seating and reception area ideal for conversation between you and your guests, the table obviously plays a central role in design and function. But again, creative thinking is key. A grand piano provides an exquisite "table" for serving after-dinner coffee. Set with a silver tray and paired with pretty linens, golden flatware, and delicate coffee cups and saucers, the impressive musical instrument draws the eye in a new and unique way.

And as with music, the concept of "variations on a theme" provides an artful sensibility to complete the scene and draw the elements together. While piping hot coffee awaits pouring on the piano, mellow, aged brandy takes center stage on a marble-topped table nearby. The arrangement of tables, chairs, and servingwares in the room allows for comfortable consumption of after-dinner beverages. And though subtle, notice how the filigreed golden rims of the cordial glasses mirror the bands of gold that encircle the coffee cups and saucers, as well as the silverware.

OPPOSITE: Fine crystal should always be hand-washed, and this is especially true when caring for gold or silver-rimmed stemware. When cleaning, use warm water—not hot—and a mild soap only. Dry with a soft, lint-free cloth and store immediately after use to avoid potential scratches or damage.

SOCIAL GRACES

A great hostess is never at a loss for something to serve when unexpected guests drop in. Lingering over a cup of coffee or a cooling glass of iced tea and a plate of sugary bites or salty nibbles is as essential to the table and the art of conversation as cup and saucer or sentence and tone. Whipping up a dazzling display in minutes is easy—all it takes is a little bit of know-how and a touch of inspiration. Then again, a few crowd-pleasing recipes don't hurt either.

OPPOSITE: I believe the most beautiful centerpieces are made of blooms freshly cut from your very own flower and herb gardens. The rosemary in this bouquet adds an aromatic touch.

{ PRETTY PRESENTATION }

A white wicker tray atop an old-fashioned picnic basket makes a whimsical impromptu serving station for two Southern classics—sweet iced tea and salty Cheddar wafers. For an updated twist on an old favorite, I like to gussy up sweet tea in its Sunday best with a simple berry syrup and a touch of tartness, using frozen lemonade concentrate. Couldn't be easier, and it's always a hit with thirsty guests.

BLACKBERRY LEMON ICED TEA
Yield: about 1 gallon

3½ quarts water, divided
3   family size tea bags
1   cup sugar
¾   cup Blackberry Simple Syrup (recipe follows)
1   (12-ounce) can frozen lemonade concentrate, thawed
Garnish: lemon slices or wedges

1. In a small pan, boil 2 cups water over high heat. Remove from heat, add tea bags, cover and steep 5 minutes; remove tea bags.
2. In a large pitcher, combine tea, sugar, and Blackberry Simple Syrup; stir until sugar is dissolved. Add lemonade concentrate and stir to mix well. Add remaining water, stirring to combine. Chill until ready to serve. Pour over ice and garnish with lemon slices or wedges if, desired.

BLACKBERRY SIMPLE SYRUP
Yield: about 1 cup

1   cup sugar
1⅓ cups water
½   pint blackberries

1. In a medium pan over medium heat bring sugar and water to simmer; simmer 5 minutes (sugar should be dissolved). Add berries and turn off heat.
2. Cool to room temperature. Strain out berries and pour into airtight bottle or jar.
Note: Simple syrup can be made up to two weeks ahead of use. If preferred, raspberries may be substituted.

Tip. Perfectly brewed tea starts with fresh water—for a consistently fresh infusion, use bottled. Most black teas or blends should steep only three to five minutes—any longer and the brew will be bitter. A trick for green tea— bring water to a boil, let it sit for two minutes, and then add to the tea leaves to begin steeping.

{ SWEET TREATS }

A cup of freshly brewed hot tea is as lonely as can be without a scone, cookie, or pastry to enjoy it with. These heart-shaped Red Velvet Scones are a special favorite of mine—they are adapted from the famous Southern cake of the same name. A cream cheese glaze drizzled over each mimics the rich frosting that makes Red Velvet Cake such a dessert table treasure in the South. No guest can resist them, or my lighter-than-air Orange Scented Madeleines.

RED VELVET SCONES WITH CREAM CHEESE GLAZE
Yield: 15 scones

2¼ cups all-purpose flour
⅔ cup sugar
¼ cup unsweetened cocoa powder
1 teaspoon baking soda
¼ teaspoon salt
½ cup unsalted butter
¾ cup plus 1 tablespoon heavy cream, divided
1 large egg
2 tablespoons red food coloring
½ teaspoon vanilla extract
Cream Cheese Glaze (recipe follows)

1. Preheat oven to 350°. Line 2 baking sheets with parchment paper.
2. In a large bowl, combine flour, sugar, cocoa, baking soda, and salt. Using a pastry blender, cut in butter until mixture is crumbly.
3. In a small bowl, whisk together ¾ cup heavy cream, egg, food coloring, and vanilla extract. Combine cream mixture and flour mixture, stirring just until dry ingredients are moistened; dough will be sticky.
4. On a lightly floured surface, roll dough to ½-inch thickness. Using a heart shaped cutter, cut scones and place on baking sheets. Brush tops evenly with 1 tablespoon heavy cream.
5. Bake 10 to 12 minutes. Cool completely. Using a pastry bag fitted with a plain tip, pipe on Cream Cheese Glaze.

Tip: Consider purchasing a set of china just for picnics. A black and white checkered pattern—one that mimics the classic gingham picnic tablecloth—holds timeless appeal and mixes and matches with any color linens or glassware.

CREAM CHEESE GLAZE
Yield: 1½ cups

1   (3-ounce) package cream cheese, softened
1   cup confectioners' sugar
1   tablespoon heavy cream

In a medium bowl, combine cream cheese, confectioners' sugar and heavy cream. Using electric mixer at low speed, beat until smooth.

ORANGE SCENTED MADELEINES
Yield: 3 dozen cookies

1   cup cake flour
½   teaspoon baking powder
¼   teaspoon salt
½   cup unsalted butter, softened
¾   cup sugar
2   large eggs
1   egg white
1   tablespoon grated orange zest
1   teaspoon orange extract
½   teaspoon French vanilla extract
Garnish: confectioners' sugar

1. Preheat oven to 325°. Spray madeleine pan with non-stick baking spray with flour.
2. In a medium bowl, sift together flour, baking powder, and salt; set aside.
3. In a separate bowl using an electric mixer at medium speed, beat butter until fluffy. Gradually add sugar and beat until light and creamy. Add eggs and egg white one at a time, beating well after each addition.
4. Add orange zest, orange extract, and French vanilla extract, beating until combined. Gradually add flour mixture, beating until well blended.
5. Spoon heaping teaspoons into each well of prepared pan. Bake 18 to 20 minutes, remove to wire rack and cool completely. Repeat with remaining batter. Sprinkle with confectioners' sugar, if desired.

{ COOLING COCKTAILS }

Though I'm not really a drinker, it pays to have a few tried-and-true cocktail recipes on-hand. A neighbor who loaned me these loves to wow her female friends with a grown-up version of a little-girl coke float. Instead of ice cream, she uses colorful sherbet, and sweet Champagne is a fizzy stand-in for the cola. And of course, sweet tea makes an appearance on the after-five beverage menu!

RASPBERRY SHERBET CHAMPAGNE FLOATS
Yield: 6-8 servings

1   (16-ounce) container frozen raspberry sherbet
1   bottle champagne
Garnish: fresh raspberries

1. Drop sherbet by tablespoonfuls into champagne flutes.
2. Add enough Champagne to fill flute.
3. Garnish with fresh raspberries, if desired.
Note: Any sherbet may be used and ginger ale can substitute for the Champagne.

SPIKED SWEET TEA
Yield: about 1 gallon

3½ quarts plus 2 cups water, divided
3   family size tea bags
1   cup sugar
¾   cup lemon flavored vodka
Garnish: lemon slices

1. In a small pan, boil 2 cups water over high heat. Remove from heat, add tea bags, cover and steep 5 minutes; remove tea bags.
2. In a large pitcher, combine tea, sugar, and remaining 3½ quarts water and stir until dissolved. Add vodka and stir to mix well. Chill until ready to serve. Garnish with lemon slices if desired.
Note: For non-drinkers, simply leave out the vodka. The result? Southern sweet tea.

{ FEEDING THE SENSES }

Building a Wardrobe for the Table

These have I loved: White plates and cups, clean-gleaming,
Ringed with blue lines; and feathery, faery dust…

—RUPERT BROOKE

When I was only 17 years old, I strolled into an antique store, took one look at a set of blue and white-patterned dinnerware and stopped still in the aisle. I immediately placed the set on lay-away and worked for months as a church pianist to pay for it. When I first spied that service for eight, I felt a purely feminine tug of longing that I have since experienced time and time again as I have grown older, as my tastes have evolved, and as my love for beautiful china has deepened. The attire for your table is as important as the apparel you wear—it is a visual statement of who you are as a woman, and like any wardrobe, your collection of table finery will take time to build. And though we all long for exclusive sets of china, collecting is not about price, it's about what excites you. Some of my most prized pieces were bargain finds! By growing your table wardrobe with an eye not just for today, but for tomorrow as well, and by cultivating your working knowledge of table and servingwares, you will learn to design eye-catching tablescapes with ease.

"MAGNOLIA AND BIRD" WATERCOLOR, BY ZEN CHUANG

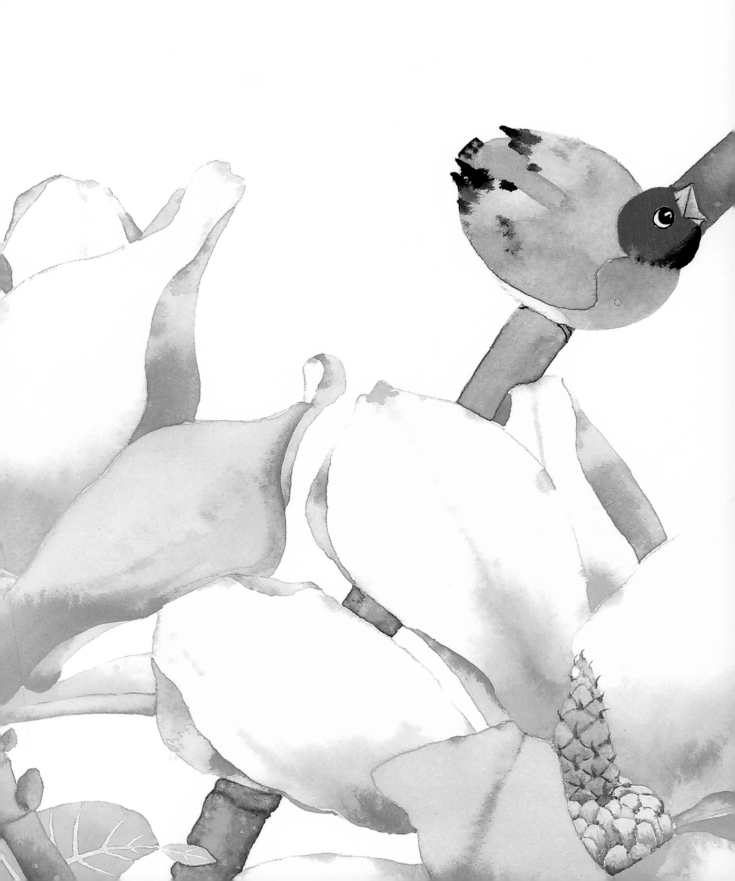

{ DINNERWARE }

Choosing china for any and all occasions is no small matter, and doing so is one of my great pleasures. Picking just the right charger to coordinate with my dinner plates, weighing whether to use my Spode or Johnson Brothers blue and white, then mixing it up just for the joy of it—such fun! No matter if you are a young about-to-be bride selecting a formal pattern for registry or a seasoned collector of beautiful tablewares, a little knowledge goes a long way in making choices that suit your tastes and lifestyle.

Dinner
9-11 inches across

Luncheon
8-9 inches across

Salad
6-8 inches across

Fish
8-9 inches across
(bears fish-patterned
ornamentation)

*Bread
& Butter*
5-7 inches across

Dessert
7.25-8.5 inches across

Tidbit
4-7 inches across

Crescent
4.5 wide, 7-8 long

Fruit Saucer
4-6 inches across, 1 inch deep

PLATES

Whether you opt for a coupe or rimmed style with a well in the center, the plates in your china pantry should include, at a minimum, pieces for serving bread and butter, salad, the main course, and dessert. Other pieces, such as a crescent or tidbit plate are lovely extras to add as your collection grows.

Soup Plate
7-10 inches across

Soup-Cereal
5.75-8.75 inches across
(rimless)

Covered Soup
4.5-6.5 inches across,
2-3.5 inches deep

Lug Soup
4-6 inches across

Cream Soup Cup
& Saucer
4-5 inches across
(double handled)

Bouillon Cup
& Saucer
3-4 inches across

BOWLS

Most five-piece place settings offer today's buyer a choice of either a bread and butter plate or a soup or cereal bowl. Though an important element of formal dining service, different styles of bowls most often must be purchased separately, so it's important to know what bowl is needed for which purpose.

While certainly decorative, the size and shape of a bowl is determined by how it is to be used and what will be served in it to diners. If you have ever had the displeasure of sipping cold soup, you understand this well. A soup plate, which is shallow, is perfect for a chunkier soup that retains its heat, but is impractical for a cream soup or consommé. A soup-cereal bowl is highly functional, but only used for more casual dining. Other types of bowls, such as the lug soup bowl, are wonderful to have in your collection, but would be out-of-place at a formal table. Lug soup bowls, for instance, are ideal both in size and depth for serving heartier fare, such as chili, thick stews and chunky chowders, and most commonly, French onion soup with melted cheese on top.

{ TIPS TO REMEMBER }

Building your china collection begins with learning the finer points of basic tablewares.

- Know the criteria for quality china. Dinnerware sets made of porcelain and bone china are among the most expensive not only because of their enduring beauty, but more importantly, because of their durability—both are more chip and break resistant than storeware, ceramics, or pottery. And don't just consider the material from which the china is made, inspect the dinner and serving pieces for defects and flaws. If plates are even slightly warped, if you see bubbles in the glaze, or if serving piece or bowl lids do not fit tightly, reconsider your choice.

- Don't just collect fine china; choose an everyday set as well for less formal occasions. Most department stores will yield numerous choices in styles for casual entertaining, from 20-piece starter sets to serving pieces to match.

- Whether you have a soft spot for pastel floral patterns or an abiding love of stark simplicity, there are china patterns in numerous sizes, shapes, and colors to choose from. If your tastes are still evolving, however, consider a simple white or cream in a classic, versatile round shape. These will not only mix and match with countless other design patterns, food always looks beautiful against a white or cream background. Take note of the china used at the next four or five-star restaurant you visit. Plates, saucers and bowls are almost always white or cream—for a reason.

- Make the commitment to buy or register for a five-piece place setting with a service for ten to twelve. This ensures that your table is perfectly set no matter the occasion, from an intimate dinner for four to a Thanksgiving meal for the entire family.

- Always hand-wash fine china in a towel-cushioned sink using a non-abrasive, mild detergent. Also, water should be warm but not hot, and dishes should be allowed to air dry before finishing the job with a soft cloth.

One should never do anything one cannot discuss at dinner.

—OSCAR WILDE

{ CRYSTAL & GLASSWARE }

The choice of available glasswares today is almost as plentiful as one's choice of china patterns. I know that in my own china pantry, there is a mix of colorful tumblers and stems, fine crystal, and everyday drinking glasses. While personal taste should be a deciding factor in making similar choices for your own collection, so should lifestyle and how well the glasswares will coordinate with your china. Decide first what you like, but consider how often you will use the pieces, whether you want primarily machine-washable glasswares, and whether you prefer plain or patterned, clear or colored.

Aperitif   White Wine   Red Wine   Claret   Water Goblet

Coupe   Tulip   Hollow Stem   Trumpet   Flute

STEMWARE

The maze of stemware choices is not merely aesthetic in nature. In fact, the shape of the glass can affect the taste of the beverage it holds. The bowl of a white wine glass, for instance, is more narrow and less shallow than a red wine glass. This releases the bouquet of a white wine more easily, while the bowl of a red wine stem allows a heavier red the room it needs to "breathe" in the glass. The variance in Champagne glasses is more decorative, though purists maintain that sparkling wine is best enjoyed in a style with a narrow rim to preserve the wine's effervescence.

{ TIPS TO REMEMBER }

Whether collected by color or pattern, glassware is an essential element of your dinnerware collection.

- Start with a basic suite of stemware, which includes a goblet, a Champagne flute, and a wine glass each for reds and whites. Add to your collection over time such pieces as iced beverage or lager glasses, cordial glasses, tumblers, sherbet and ice cream dishes, as well as decanters and pitchers—all are part of your wardrobe of glasswares.

- Some basic style choices to consider when collecting fine crystal are plain, cut or etched, and banded, which has precious metal such as gold or platinum on the rim.

- Make sure your collection includes not only crystal, but also durable, sturdy glass drinkingwares for everyday use. A standard set of 12-ounce glasses will yield numerous uses.

- When purchasing a set of glasswares, always pick up one or two extra glasses in case of breakage.

- Colored glasswares are eye-popping on the table, but less practical than clear crystal or glass, which will match anything. Weave these special pieces into your collection as it grows.

- Inspect crystal glasswares before purchase. Hold a stemmed piece and lightly tap the bowl of the glass. Do you hear a bell-like tone? That's a good sign. Now, hold the piece against a white background—the clearer the crystal the higher its quality. Hold it. Does the piece feel heavier than glass? That's the lead content, and, again, it signifies quality.

- Never place crystal in a dishwasher, and wash carefully—it scratches easily. Wash in lukewarm water with a mild detergent, and rinse in water with a bit of vinegar added—this helps keep the shine brilliant. For cut or etched crystal pieces, use a soft toothbrush, and, unlike dinnerwares, don't allow crystal pieces to air dry, as this method encourages water spots. Dry with a soft, lint-free cloth and store pieces upright in a cool area.

Let me sip from the goblet of worth.

—SEAN KIRKPATRICK CLANCY

{ STERLING SILVER }

Though it is sometimes overlooked, flatware says as much about the look and design of a table as the choice of china. In fact, many experts and registry consultants will urge you to choose your silverware first, then find a china pattern that complements the flatware. Seems a little oversimplified to my thinking, because if you're like me, your sets of china will grow exponentially over time, and your silverware will be called upon to match each and every one! Rather than be hemmed in by a single pattern, I just buy what I love and find a way to work it into my collection.

{ TIPS TO REMEMBER }

To set a table with real silver, every fork and spoon in place, is not only to create a beautiful table, but also to take part in timeless tradition.

- Sterling silver remains the standard for flatware, but in today's market, one is likely to find a beautiful array of options in silverplate, which is less expensive, but which can also lack a certain "heirloom" quality. Real sterling must be a minimum of 92.5 percent silver and should be stamped "sterling" to indicate its quality.

- No matter your criteria for choice of patterns, be sure you select silverware that is comfortable to hold and is made with a design that speaks to you in some fashion. A five-place setting—a dinner and salad fork, dinner knife, soup spoon and teaspoon—with service for eight to twelve is sufficient to begin your collection, along with a hostess set for serving. The pieces in a hostess may vary, and can include a cold meat fork, a serving spoon, a slotted serving spoon, a pastry server, a gravy ladle, and a butter serving knife.

- Round out your silver collection with such pretty pieces as candlestick holders, tea sets, coffee pots, salvers, and other serving pieces. Auctions and estate sales are great for finding just such items.

- Consider purchasing a second set of flatware for more casual dining. For this set, stainless steel is a perfectly acceptable choice, and happily, is dishwasher safe!

- Don't make the mistake of locking away your silver and never using it. Constant wear actually improves the look of silver, and minimizes the need to polish. When using at meals, however, remember that salt and certain foods will promote tarnishing—such as eggs, vinegar, mayonnaise, and tomatoes—so wash the pieces quickly after contact.

- One caveat about washing silver—don't use lemon-scented detergents, and always let your silver air-dry before storing. These steps help prevent tarnishing.

- Both sterling and silverplate should be stored in an airtight chest or cupboard, each piece individually wrapped in flatware rolls or other tarnish-resistant cloth. Take the time at least once or twice a year to polish your silver. Your gleaming table will thank you for it with every use.

One of a belle's most important duties in life is choosing a silver pattern.

—CAROLYN KENT

Tomato
Server

Jelly
Trowel

Nut
Pick

Lettuce
Fork

Sugar
Shifter

Marrow
Spoon

Soup
Ladle

Lemon
Fork

Olive
Fork

Petit Four
Scoop

ESTATE SERVERS

One of my favorite ways to spend a Saturday morning is to hit the antique store trail or scour flea markets in search of silver estate serving pieces. I like to think of these pieces not as "must-haves," but "should-haves." Not only are such utensils unique and exquisite, but quite often are also ingenious additions to the table. As functional as they are collectible, estate servers round out a well-set table, adding sophistication and an undeniable note of elegance.

{ FINE LINENS }

Like most women I know, I simply adore linens on the table. The endless parade of colors, textures, and patterns bring such versatility to the design scheme, changing the entire look with a mere switch of the placemats.

What's more, a table dressed with fine linens is one that proclaims unmistakable polish. From monogrammed napkins that personalize to a fine damask tablecloth that adds a layer of elegance, linens are one of the most basic elements of the table trousseau, and one of the most important.

{ TIPS TO REMEMBER }

From table runners to place mats, an ensemble of quality linens is fundamental to the well-dressed table.

- Before choosing any linen, your first task is to measure your dining and breakfast tables. An overhang of three to eight inches on all sides is customary. Round or square cloths can work on round tables, but square or rectangular tables are prettiest with cloths of the same shape. Another consideration: If your dining room table has leaves, be sure you have tablecloths that accommodate the table with or without the addition of the leaves.

- Your ensemble of basic linens should begin with a formal and a casual tablecloth, dinner and luncheon napkins with coordinating napkin rings, placemats, at least one table runner, and a silence cloth. Extras, such as toppers, tray and center cloths, sideboard scarves, cruet mats, and carving cloths are lovely additions to collect as you go.

- For those just beginning to accrue a wardrobe of linens, start with lace, linen, or damask pieces in ivory or cream. These basic colors will match practically all tablewares, and will never go out of style—they're considered classics for a reason.

- Consider monogramming at least one set of white linens, either in the single or three-letter style—whatever your preference. Tablecloths are usually monogrammed either in the center, on all four or two diagonal corners; placemats in the lower right corner; and napkins in the center or lower right corner. The unwaning appeal of monograms speaks to the artfulness of this seemingly simple embellishment.

- If you crave color, choose an undercloth in a solid hue and a topper in a coordinating color or pattern. The layered effect adds intensity and tone.

- I suggest you launder your own linens, washing and pressing them before storing. To avoid creases and rot, store linens wrapped around cardboard tubes that have been covered with acid-free tissue or just-laundered muslin. If you prefer to hang linens, make sure the hanger is covered to protect the cloth. Also if you are laundering rarely used linens before a big event, try this time-saving trick. Place freshly laundered, still slightly damp linens in the freezer. When you are ready to place them on the table, remove, and iron to creaseless perfection!

A napkin is a graceful auxiliary in the process of a meal and not rather an embarrassing superfluity of furtive application.

—GEORGE GISSING

{ SERVING PIECES }

218

A suite of serving pieces that matches the pattern of your dinnerware is often called a "completer set." I have always felt this is an apt term, as indeed, these pieces complete the look of a lovely table and make wonderful inheritance pieces to hand down from one generation to the next. One of the most treasured servingwares in my own collection is a vegetable bowl that belonged to my grandmother, a piece she received at her own wedding. This treasured heirloom makes me wax nostalgic for my grandmother, who always filled that bowl with her best dishes, especially the vegetables grown fresh in her garden. When I place the bowl on my own table, there is indeed a sense of completeness, one that transcends time.

{ TIPS TO REMEMBER }

Serving pieces provide finish and polish to the well-set table.

- Make your servingwares perform double duty at the table by using them in centerpieces. A pretty pitcher looks lovely filled with long-stemmed flowers, while a shallow bowl showcases a close-clipped bouquet. Mismatched sugar pots and creamers are just the right size for a linear display of flowers in the center of the table. And think beyond flowers. A silver salver arranged with an assortment of delicate, colorful perfume bottles is a unique centerpiece for a smaller table, and a cut-crystal trifle or punch bowl needs only a white pillar candle or a jumble of Christmas ornaments to lend glow and warmth to the table.

- A basic set of servingwares should include beverage pitchers, a large and medium oval platter, a vegetable bowl, a gravy boat or saucière and stand, a covered casserole dish, a cake plate, a salad bowl, salt and pepper shakers, a butter dish, and a sugar and creamer set. Other pieces to incorporate into your collection as it grows are three-tiered trays, decanters, chafing dishes, soup tureens, trifle bowls, compotes, bread trays, cheese boards, nut or tidbit dishes, cruet sets, teapots, coffee pots, and chocolate pots.

- Some types of holloware can be difficult to distinguish, especially when you discover single pieces in antique stores, flea markets, and estate sales. Coffee pots and chocolate pots are very similar, but a chocolate pot is typically a bit smaller with a shorter spout that is higher up on the body. Another difference: you will often find a filter over the inside opening of a coffee pot's spout. Teapots are the most easily distinguished. They are shorter with a rounded body. This is deliberate in the design, as it allows room in the pot for tea leaves to expand during infusion.

- Purchase both shallow and deep serving bowls—both are necessary for any number of uses at the table. Deeper bowls are just right for salads and softer side dishes, such as rice, potatoes, or any vegetable that is served in its own liquid. A deeper bowl preserves the food's heat while accommodating a serving spoon. More shallow bowls are ideal for grilled or roasted vegetables, fresh or cooked fruit, or dinner rolls.

A table, a chair, a bowl of fruit and a violin, what else does a man need to be happy?

—ALBERT EINSTEIN

{ REWARDING THE EYES }

Embellishing with Flair

…Our desires, our food, are all really necessary for our existence in the first instance. But the rose is an extra. Its smell and its colour are an embellishment of life, not a condition of it. It is only goodness which gives extras.

—SIR ARTHUR CONAN DOYLE

A table without flowers is one that seems bare to my eyes. Their ethereal allure brings a note of softness and color to the overall design scheme, offering infinite options in color, shape, and form. But flowers are only one embellishment that adds life to your tablescape, and make no mistake about it, such details are not mere gilding on the lily—they complete the picture. The dinnerware pattern may be divine and the silverware polished to a gleaming patina, but it is the one-of-a-kind accents bearing your personal stamp that truly tie the look together. I like to be daring when decorating my table. Flowers are a must, but I feel that inherited family treasures, knick-knacks, and curios I've collected over the years are as beautiful displayed on the dining table as they are elsewhere in my home. It is these kinds of inspired choices that make others wish they had thought of it first, and leave your guests inspired and renewed when they sit at the table. "MAGNOLIA AND BIRD" WATERCOLOR, BY ZEN CHUANG

{ ARTFUL FLOWERS }

Flowers are as universal, as elemental, as love. Whether sitting pretty on a table, tendril-twining about a garden gate, or pressed between the pages of a favorite book, flowers possess a nuance of color, scent, and shape that makes each bloom in the bunch seem a creation of divine perfection. A vase overflowing with a lovely arrangement holds the almost magical ability to beckon us to the table, then captivate us once we're there. When it comes to crafting your own arrangements for centerpieces or decorative table accents, you need not be an expert floral designer, you need only gather your favorite flowers and a few supplies and let your creativity soar.

NATURAL BEAUTY

From loose buds in a pitcher to single stems in a glass, remember when working with flowers and greenery that unless you have experience or training in floral design, it's fine to keep it simple; your table will be just as beautiful as a result. Be creative, find the right container—one that suits the arrangement, occasion, and tablescape design—and let the natural beauty of the flowers do all the work.

{ FAMILY HEIRLOOMS }

Regardless of their appraised worth, the sets of china, silver, and crystal, passed from parent to child are true treasures, because this act ensures these heirlooms will survive yet another generation. With every use, these precious pieces tell the story of who we are and where we came from, illustrating our personal and family histories and serving as vivid reminders of some our most cherished memories. If teacups could talk, what stories they would tell!

{ MONOGRAMS }

Whether your own monogram or an eclectic collection of acquired pieces, the simple embellishment of initialing is not just lovely on linens, it adds elegance to fine china as well. Customizing dinnerwares in this fashion adds decoration to the pattern and truly makes every meal for which it is used a celebration of history and heritage. What's more, when these pieces are used, their very presence provides accent and ornamentation, minimizing the need for decorative accessories. At a small, four-person table or a larger table that is dominated by a stately floral centerpiece, this can be ideal. Consider these tips for personalizing your own pieces.

- Monogrammed china must be specially commissioned, and you will be asked to choose from any number of colors and fonts. Choose one that suits both the china and your personal sense of style.

- For a traditional three-letter monogram, the center initial is largest and represents the last name. The groom's first name initial is placed to the right and the bride's to the left. The woman's full name may also be used, with her first name initial on the right and her middle name on the left.

- Have a set of chargers monogrammed with a single initial in the top center of the plate's rim.

- Look in antique stores for monogrammed pieces. My friend Betty Kitchings received a set from her aunt in just this way. However, it is not Betty's full initials on the pieces, only the last K in the center. Her aunt knew Betty loved monograms, so when she found a superb set, she snapped it up. I feel the same. A beautifully hand-painted set with great scrollwork would be attractive on anyone's table. You could always fib and say the monogram is that of a great-aunt on your father's side!

{ CHARMING COLLECTIBLES }

There is a long-standing Christmas tradition in my home, one that is deeply tender to me. Each year, the unpacking of the ceramic crèche is a revered ritual with my sons and husband. The Nativity scene figures were created and hand-painted by my mother many years ago, and given to me. The central piece, the manger, was crafted by my Daddy, made from wood and sticks he collected from our yard. Today, when I unpack those pieces with my family, and arrange each one just so, with every gesture I am reminded of my life—as it was, as it is, and as I hope it will be. Such pieces are even more beautiful because they are imprinted with remembrance of the moments you have shared with those dearest to your heart, and speak to the mutual milestones to come.

CHRISTMAS COLOR

There is no holiday I can think of that beckons more to dynamic color and decoration than Christmas. Tradition, naturally, is also an important element of a Noel-themed design scheme. This is especially true for a seasonal dining table. Using a central theme, such as color or motif, mingle family heirlooms and holiday decorations accrued over time with more recently acquired accessories—candle-holders, flowers, garlands of evergreen, and more. The result is a breathtaking mix of old and new.

SEASONAL CENTERPIECE

The centerpiece of a table is naturally the visual focus, and the perfect opportunity to use your prettiest holiday decorations. With the table seen here, miniature faux Christmas trees are balanced in both shape and height by a collection of pretty ornaments. A swathe of glittering fabric is a natural nest for the ornaments, and lends a hint of softness.

{ UNEXPECTED TREASURES }

Let me tell you a little secret—and bear in mind, this is strictly classified information in the (as yet) unwritten rule book for Southern ladies. Being a bit unpredictable is not only wise; it's just plain fun. How does this translate to the table? For me, it means taking elements from the here and now and putting them front and center. If I am inspired by the russet shades of autumn in October, then visitors might find a display of leaves and acorns on my table. If, in April, the simple newness of spring renews me in spirit, my guests are likely to discover at my table little treasures that echo the spark in spring that makes it a season like no other. These kinds of subtle and unexpected flourishes make your table more beautiful, and certainly more interesting, by expanding the confines of tradition just enough to accommodate a bit of mood and whimsy.

{ UNUSUAL ACCENTS }

Unusual accents bring more to the table than form, shape, and color. Curios and collectibles are also fabulous conversation starters that beg guests to ask where you got them, who gave them to you, and so on. This, in turn, affords you the opening to reminisce about your friends, your travels, and your adventures. Consider these suggestions in introducing the unusual into your table designs:

- Fill a trifle bowl with almost anything that strikes your fancy—colorful tea towels, fresh or faux fruit, Christmas ornaments…the list is endless.

- Precious figurines are as lovely on the table as they are in your curio cabinet—use them in numerous styles and contexts.

- Crystal or glass flower vases can stand alone as decoration if used in a way that flatters their shape, color, and style.

- Fill assorted apothecary jars with whole pieces of fruit, then arrange by size and shape.

- Use tole-painted metal or wooden containers as a base for simple yet stunning centerpieces. These work especially well with Early American or Victorian-style design schemes.

- Use seasonal produce in interesting ways, such as a single pear resting in a sherbet glass or an antique compote. Berries, plums, persimmons, Seckel pears, kumquats, grapes—these are just a few fruits that are as beautiful as they are delicious. Use them bountifully at the table when they are in season.

- Incorporate anything you collect and love into your table design. Antique books can be stacked in the center of the table and used as the base for a centerpiece. Vintage perfume bottles and atomizers arranged in a mirrored underplate make a lovely centerpiece as well. I know a woman who collects antique and unusual buttons. At a dinner I attended in her home, she had created charming chargers by attaching the buttons in a decorative fashion.

Charm is more than just beauty

—YIDDISH
PROVERB

{ FINISHING TOUCHES }

Someone once said that God is in the details, and I know it's true. It's the details that dazzle us the most, the little "I-can't-believe-you-thought-of-it" touches that make everything a little more special, whether it's the garnish on an already divine tea sandwich or a sweet little extra on the table that elevates the look from finished to polished.

NAPKIN ACCENTS

If you entertain often, you invariably draw the same group of guests at one point or another. To keep your table looking fresh, especially as your china collection grows, change the look of your table with a simple switch of napkin rings. Whether purchased or whipped up in a jiffy with a snippet of ribbon and pretty charm attached, this small touch will have a huge impact.

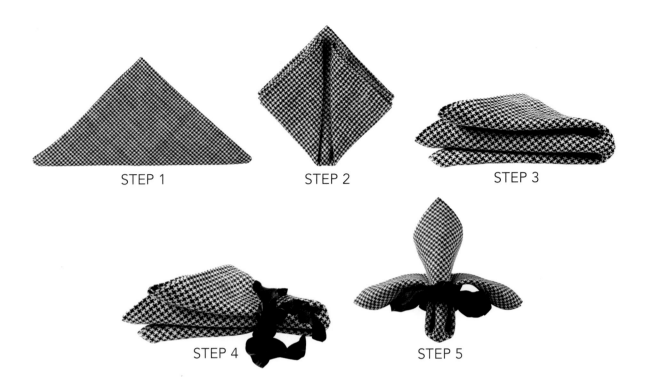

STEP 1

STEP 2

STEP 3

STEP 4

STEP 5

NAPKIN FOLDING

The etiquette of napkin placement has changed over time, from somewhat rigid rules to more relaxed guidelines that have opened the doors to creative napkin folding and display. Follow these step-by-step instructions for a charming fleur-de-lis patterned napkin, followed by a simple but lovely design.

STEP 1: For this design, begin with a heavier-weave napkin, or use one that has been starched. With the napkin lying flat, fold it in half diagonally, forming a large triangle with the point at the top.

STEP 2: Fold the bottom right point in to meet the top point. Repeat the same on the left, bringing the left point to the top center point.

STEP 3: Holding the napkin at the top and bottom points, pick it up, fold it in half again and let the points fall to the bottom. Lay the napkin down with the long edge toward you.

STEP 4: Loosely tie a ribbon around the bottom third of the folded napkin.

STEP 5: Prop the napkin up on the right edge of the triangle. Let the outside folds of the napkin fall to the sides, and fluff the middle fold until it is full and stands upright.

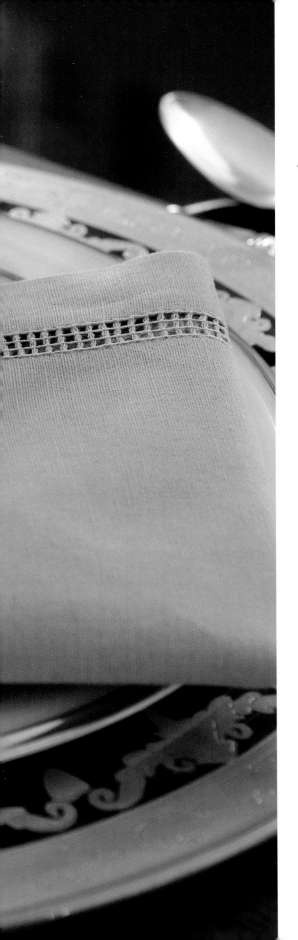

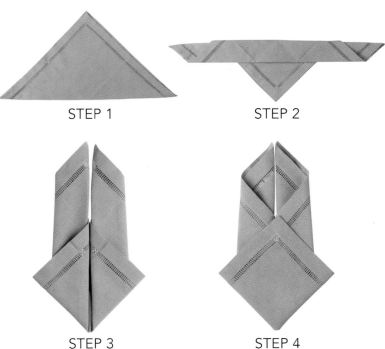

STEP 1   STEP 2

STEP 3   STEP 4

STEP 1: With the napkin lying flat, fold it in half diagonally forming a large triangle with the point at the top. Fold this point down to meet the bottom edge of the triangle, and finger press this fold. Open the fold, returning the napkin to the triangle shape.

STEP 2: Fold the bottom edge of the triangle up about two inches and finger press the fold. Repeating this exact movement, fold the "new" edge up about two inches, ending with two folds. The folds should meet the crease you made in Step 1. Flip it to the position shown.

STEP 3: Hold the middle of the top of the napkin with your left thumb and forefinger. Without breaking the straight edge, bring the right point in and down, until it is dividing the bottom of the triangle directly in half through the point. Switch hands and repeat with left point. Keeping it flat, rotate the napkin so that the diamond shape is pointing down.

STEP 4: Finally, simply flip the napkin over so that the bottom of the napkin is a smooth diamond shape with no folds visible.

LIGHTING

Though it is often overlooked as a "finishing touch," ambient lighting is one of the most important elements of a successful tablescape. Too-dim lighting can leave guests fumbling for silverware, while lighting that is too bright can make the table look garish and your guests uncomfortable—as though they are sitting in an unwanted spotlight. Candles always help strike a happy medium with overhead lights, adding a bit of brightness and warmth that relaxes everyone and casts a golden glow over the table.

{ RESOURCES }

To find items featured throughout the book, please refer to the list below. Pieces not listed are either privately owned, antiques, or are no longer in production.

{ LINENS }
PREPARING THE TABLE

Page 36: Tablecloth and doilies, Martha Lauren's Antique Linens & Accessories (205.871.2283).

Page 40: Napkins, Beverly Ruff Antiques and Accessories (205.262.9434).

Page 42: Lace pillows, bedspread, Martha Lauren's Antique Linens and Accessories (205.871.2283).

Page 52: Organdy tablecloth, Martha Lauren's Antique Linens and Accessories (205.871.2283).

Page 63: Napkins, Christine's (205.871.8297).

Page 80: Placemat, At Home Furnishings *www.athome-furnishings.com.*

Page 86: Tablecloth, Pier 1 Imports *www.pier1.com.*

Page 90 and 92: Napkins, At Home Furnishings *www.athome-furnishings.com.*

Page 102: Lace placemats, Martha Lauren's Antique Linens & Accessories (205.871.2283).

Page 106: Tablecloth and napkins, Martha Lauren's Antique Linens & Accessories (205.871.2283).

Page 112: Napkins, Table Matters *www.table-matters.com.*

Page 145: Napkins, Table Matters *www.table-matters.com.*

Page 148: Napkins, Lamb's Ears Ltd. *www.lambsearsbham.com.*

Page 157: Napkins, Christine's (205.871.8297). Throw, Anthropologie *www.anthropologie.com.*

Page 171: Napkins, Martha Lauren's Antique Linens & Accessories (205.871.2283).

FEEDING THE SENSES

Page 211: Linens, Martha Lauren's Antique Linens & Accessories (205.871.2283).

Page 215 and 216: Linens, Martha Lauren's Antique Linens & Accessories (205.871.2283).

REWARDING THE EYES

Page 234: Napkins, Lamb's Ears Ltd. *www.lambsearsbham.com.*

Page 238: Linens, Harmony Landing, (205.871.0585).

{ CRYSTAL AND GLASSWARE }
PREPARING THE TABLE

Page 36: Gold rimmed glasses, Gorham *www.gorham1831.com.*

Page 52: Tall glasses, Lamb's Ears Ltd. *www.lambsearsbham.com.*

Page 63: Glasses, World Market *www.worldmarket.com.*

Page 67: Parfait glasses, At Home Furnishings *www.athome-furnishings.com.*

Page 87: Tall cylinder glasses, Pier 1 Imports *www.pier1.com.*

Page 90: Blue stemware, Artland *www.artlandinc.com.*

Page 106: Red crystal glasses, and tall Castlemaine crystal glasses, Waterford *www.waterford.com.*

Page 108: Crystal glasses, Lismore by Waterford *www.waterford.com.*

Page 110: Crystal sherbet dishes, Camelot by Stuart.

Page 112: Goblets and tall glasses, Table Matters *www.table-matters.com.*

Page 116: All crystal, Waterford *www.waterford.com.*

Page 120: Crystal, Power Court by Waterford *www.waterford.com.*

Page 145: Crystal, William Yeoward from Table Matters *www.table-matters.com.*

Page 148: Pitcher and glasses, Anthropologie *www.anthropologie.com.*

Page 165: Clear glasses, Anthropologie *www.anthropologie.com.* Striped glasses, MacKenzie-Childs *www.mackenzie-childs.com.*

Page 167: Green crystal pieces, Fostoria *www.fostoriacrystal.com.*

Page 185: Pitcher, glasses, cakestand, Anthropologie *www.anthropologie.com.*

Page 190: Both glasses, French Country by Lenox *www.lenox.com.*

FEEDING THE SENSES

Page 195: Blue crystal stemware, Bromberg's *www.brombergs.com.*

REWARDING THE EYES

Page 235: Lismore goblets and wine decanter, Waterford *www.waterford.com.* Red goblets, Lamb's Ears Ltd. *www.lambsearsbham.com.*

Page 238: Goblets, Harmony Landing (205.871.0585).

{ STERLING SILVER }
THE SOUTHERN LADY AT HOME

Page 21: Square salad container, At Home Furnishings *www.athome-furnishings.com.* Spaghetti dish, Pottery Barn *www.potterybarn.com.*

Page 23: Plate, At Home Furnishings *www.athome-furnishings.com.*

Page 31: Casserole dish, Flora (205.871.4004.)

Pages 34, 192, 222: "Magnolia and Bird" watercolor, by Zen Chuang, a physician painter whose medical practice and artwork seek to "paint our days with colors, fill our lives with beauty!" *www.FromEarthToSky.com*